FALLING INTO PLACE
Healing Through
Connecting

FALLING
INTO
PLACE
Healing Through Connecting

MARIE NEUMEIER RIENTORD

OSO Publishing Company
Springerville, Arizona

For contact information: www.rancholapuente.com

The author of this book does not dispense medical advice nor prescribe
the use of any technique as a form of treatment for medical problems
without the advice of a physician. The intent of the author is only to offer
information of a general nature to help you in your quest for emotional and
spiritual well-being. In the event you use any of the information in this book
for yourself, it is at your discretion and your sole responsibility. The author
and publisher assume no responsibility for your actions.

Excerpts from *The Pleiadian Workbook* by Amorah Quan Yin, © 1996,
Bear & Company, Rochester, VT, www.InnerTraditions.com. Used with
permission.

Cover design by Tricia Legault and Jann DeFord

Cover photo by Tom Patterson

Falling Into Place: Healing Through Connecting
Marie Neumeier Rientord
ISBN: 1453772820
Library of Congress Control Number: 2010912341

OSO Publishing Company, P.O. Box 1686, Springerville, AZ 85938
Printed in the United States of America

CONTENTS

In Gratitude

To Jann, for walking with me in wisdom, clarity, and supportive love as she became the constant eyes and ears in the birthing of each chapter of this book.

To Victor, for supporting and believing in me and in this book long before I knew there was a book, and during each season of its creation.

To Steve, my editor, for sharing his unique, enthusiastic combination of professional knowledge and spiritual understanding in urging this book on to publication.

To Lord Maitreya, for his constant inspiration and encouragement that made the birthing of this book possible.

To Lord Kuthumi, for his patient and loving guidance as I take steps on my spiritual path that I am privileged to share with others.

To my community of clients, students, family, and friends, for journeying with me each day into a deeper flow of connecting.

To Oso, who taught me how to feel unconditional love for all beings.

Introduction

We are all connected. We have been connected in oneness from the beginning of the cosmos. We are connected to all beings in our world, in our solar system, and in our universe. We are connected to all parts of ourselves, to our families, to our friends, and to our enemies. We are connected to every person we pass on the street, to every animal that lives on Mother Earth, and to Mother Earth herself.

That we are all totally connected in oneness is a very difficult concept for many of us to grasp because we live in a civilization rooted in separateness. Many of us feel separate from God, or Divine Source. We feel separate from others, separate from ourselves, and definitely separate from the rest of the cosmos. These feelings of separation lead us into tremendous fear, aggressive competition, and horrific wars. They have caused violence and struggle, hopelessness and despair. In a world of plenty, we have become financially bankrupt with astronomical numbers of people living in hunger and poverty.

You may be experiencing fears about losing money and work as economic conditions worsen and businesses and institutions collapse. You may also be experiencing deep personal traumas as fires, floods, hurricanes, and other earth changes sweep our planet. In your personal life, you may be experiencing more turmoil. Old emotional pain you thought was long gone may be resurfacing for you.

What is this all about, and what is really going on in our world and in our personal lives? Our world is experiencing a time of deep cleansing and healing. Mother Earth and all beings living on her are going through this time of upheaval and change in order to move into the next cycle of time and energy within our solar system, our galaxy, and our universe. Our earth is moving into the Age of Light, culminating with the end of the Mayan Calendar at the Winter Solstice in 2012.

This new cycle is unlike any that has come before it on earth. Moving into the Age of Light means that Mother Earth is ascending. She is moving into a higher consciousness than she has ever before experienced as a third-dimensional solid planet in our solar system. Mother Earth is moving into the higher-dimensional consciousness of flowing, harmony, and oneness. And as human beings living on the earth, we have the chance to ascend with her! We can choose to move with her into this new age of deep connectedness, sharing, and peace.

Whenever Mother Earth moves into a new cycle of time and energy within our galaxy, all negative forms and energy from the previous cycle must be cleansed. In this current cycle, all institutions that carry the negativity of greed and corruption must fall. They will be replaced with new structures that are filled with the light of justice and sharing. Creating those light-filled structures is essential for our next big leap in carrying out the Divine Plan for all creation.

In order to prepare for such a momentous event, we humans are also going through deep cleansing in physical, emotional, mental, and spiritual ways. Our bodies are expanding to allow in tremendous amounts of light. Our darkness of fear and struggle, which has been so much a part of this cycle, is beginning to open to the light. We are finally beginning to learn that feeling separate is an illusion we need not accept. In fact, our very healing is based on the Divine truth that we are one; we will heal our bodies, our minds, our families, and our earth through connecting.

The story of my healing work with others is the story of my own healing journey. In 1962, when I was 20 years old and teaching children, I realized that my own Inner Child needed healing. I didn't know how to do that healing then, but I began searching for those ways. I somehow knew that by finding ways to help myself heal I would help children and other people heal as well.

For the next 20 years, my own healing path was interwoven with my work of teaching and school counseling. Whatever I learned personally, I taught to children, teenagers, and adults. Whatever I healed in myself, I helped others to heal. I learned to connect with and heal my own Inner Child. I learned to connect more deeply with people, with spiritual light beings, and with Mother Earth.

Master Kuthumi, a spiritual light being who has lived on the earth many times, became my spiritual teacher during those years. I learned to communicate with him through channeling, and he led me step-by-step as I pursued my higher purpose of healing work. Later, Lord Maitreya, another spiritual light being who is head of the Spiritual Hierarchy for this planet, began guiding me and told me that he would help me write this book.

In 1982 I began working as a psychotherapist in the San Diego area. Victor, to whom I was married at the time, suggested that I name my business "The Bridging Institute." He said that my whole life was about helping people create bridges— bridges within themselves and bridges between themselves and others. Victor and I also began looking for land where we could build a healing center. It would be a place where people could go apart for a while to create those bridges within themselves.

Today, 26 years later, Victor lives on that land. My partner, Jann, and I also live on that land. We work there in community with Victor to provide a special place where people can easily feel connecting energy within themselves, with others, and with Mother Earth. We have created "Rancho La Puente" in New Mexico. *La Puente* means "the bridge" in Spanish, and our land truly is that connecting bridge.

The name of this book came one day during a healing gathering at Rancho La Puente. At one point during Victor's healing session, he said, "If I could come into balance, then everything in my life would fall into place." Later that night Jann said that when she heard those words, she knew that this book should be named *Falling into Place: Healing Through Connecting*.

This title, which definitely came from the inspiration of Jann's Higher Self, is truly what this book is about. Our place on this earth is to remember our connectedness to Divine Source and to all beings. Feeling connected heals the woundedness that comes when we feel separated from ourselves, from people, from the earth, or from Divine Source.

When we are deep in the pain of feeling separate, we feel out of place where we are. We may feel out of place at work, where we live, or in our relationships. It may seem that there is no group we can join that is right for us. Some of us feel out of place in our own skin.

As we find ways to feel connected, we heal the emotional pain that we have been dragging around for so long. This book is a sharing of ways to heal by feeling connected to ourselves and to all other beings. As we do so, we release the illusion of separateness and fall into the place where we have always belonged. We need never feel out of place again.

Enjoy your time within the chapters of this book. They are meant to come to you gently and speak to you lovingly. I have designed them to be read and to be used as a workbook. Each chapter stands alone, with questions for reflection and a meditation to focus on one aspect of connecting. You may read the book and reflect on all the ideas I have presented here, or you may find particular chapters that speak to you and will support you in feeling connected at this time of your healing journey. Your Higher Self will guide you to receive from the book exactly what you need to receive at this time on your connecting journey.

You may find some of the chapters to be challenging, or some of the chapters may not attract you. I encourage you to read with openness, just allowing the pages to open themselves to you. The messages that you need to hear will connect with you. As you allow your Higher Self to guide you lovingly through these pages, I trust that you will *fall into place*, the unique connecting place that is yours today.

CHAPTER ONE

Inner Child Healing — Connecting with the Present

Feeling "separate" within ourselves is one of the most difficult illusions for us as human beings to release. The deep pain that it brings can last for many lifetimes. It causes us to feel out of place in many ways in our daily lives. Many of us have been so deeply wounded in the past that part of us still lives in the past without even being aware of it. We run away from the present, thinking that our present life is causing the pain. In fact, learning to come back to the present is one of the most important ways to heal the old pain.

One morning as I was preparing to write this chapter, Master Kuthumi came through with the following teaching: *Good morning, my child. I am here this morning to speak about connecting with life **every day** you are living on this planet Earth. You, the people of Earth, spend lots of time running away from life. We in the spiritual realms have some understanding of that phenomenon because we have watched and studied your way when you have pain. One of the ways you try to help yourselves feel better is by trying to run away from life. But life is in this very moment as you are reading these words. Life is in the moment you open your window to* *let in the morning sun. Life is in your drive to work in the morning. Be in those moments, connected to those moments. Many drivers in your cities become very angry with other drivers on their way to work each day. They are not feeling connected to life in that moment. They are running away from life as it is; they are running into the pent up anger and resentment they carry from the past, allowing it to boil over into their driving every day. For many of you, when you open the window to let in the morning sun, your minds are already many miles away in the past or the future, trying to run away from problems in the present. What you think of as the present is not the present at all. It is an accumulation of negative energy that you carry around with you, not knowing how to release it. One of the most important ways to release it is to* **come back to the present***, to feel connected with life in this very instant. True, you have many responsibilities each day. But those responsibilities can be made simpler if you return to the present moment over and over again each day. We are watching and sending you energy from the spiritual realms to support you in feeling connected with yourselves, with your world, with us, and with life in each moment. I send you love and light this morning.*

Some people struggle to feel connected with life in the present moment, yet they intuitively know that feeling connected and present is what authentic love is all about. As they release pain from the past, they gradually learn to live in the present moment in their daily lives.

Many people, however, show little awareness of what living in the present moment means. They act almost entirely under the influence of the past without conscious awareness that they are not living in the present. By living in the past, it becomes very easy for human beings to accumulate negative energy as a reaction to pain. Once they are caught in a cycle of negativity, it can become very difficult to release. Negativity causes feelings of separateness within, which easily lead to experiences of depression, resentment, anger, fear, and worry. I have found that one of the best ways to heal past pain and to come back to the present is to do Inner Child healing.

> *By living in the past, it becomes very easy for human beings to accumulate negative energy as a reaction to pain.*

A client named John came to me because he had lost his job three months before and had plunged into a deep depression. It brought to his mind all the jobs he had lost in the past, and he felt worthless and unable to see any of the talents and skills he possessed that could bring him money in the future. The more he looked at his past failures, the more negative he became in his relationships with his wife, his children, and his friends.

At first his friends called him to offer their support. But every time they offered support, John would respond with negative and attacking remarks, such as, "Sure, it's easy for you to feel that way. You're working! Let's see what you say when you lose your job!" Over time the friends stopped calling and stopped offering their words of encouragement, support, and love. Even his family was affected by his negativity. Whenever his wife tried to talk to him about anything concerning family needs, he told her she would have to take care of everything herself. He also told his children they could not make any noise in the house when he was home so that he could watch television. His wife felt alone and his children avoided coming home after school.

After working with John for some time, he slowly began allowing himself to feel and express the pain of failure he had carried for many years. As he expressed the pain, he realized that he had felt the pain long before adulthood. It was the pain of his Inner Child who never felt he could do anything as well as other children. As he expressed the pain and negativity he had carried for so many years, John learned to love his Inner Child and heal the separateness he had always felt within. His negativity began to dissolve.

As he continued working to heal his Inner Child, John was able to get in touch with what he truly wanted to do in the present. He was able to see, for the first time, that the work he had done in the past was not his heart's desire for this period in his life. He saw that he had chosen his past jobs mainly for the sake of supporting his family. He felt that he could never make enough money doing what he really wanted to do.

Speaking to his wife about what he now saw as the next step in his life purpose allowed John to begin communicating with her in a new and exciting way. He began creating the work he truly wanted to do, and today is running his own business and is financially stable. John is now able to live much of the time in the present moment, enjoying his relationships and supporting his family to follow *their* own dreams in life.

Many people spend much of their energy numbing their feelings of pain from childhood. Much of my daily work with clients involves helping them to talk about and access past experiences of pain. Although challenging, this process is essential in order for them to fully express and release the pain. The most successful method I have found to facilitate this process is called Inner Child healing work.

> *As we express the pain and negativity*
> *we have carried for so many years,*
> *we learn to love our Inner Child and*
> *heal the separateness we have*
> *always felt within.*

Inner Child healing work is based on the premise that we each have within our personality a part of us that is still the loving, creative, and innocent child that came into this world at birth. For most of us, the child part of our personality has been wounded through painful experiences of the past. Our childhood pain is the pain of our abandonment. Many of us were abandoned by significant people who were responsible for our well-being and growth. We may have been left through actual physical abandonment or by physical or emotional neglect. We may have been abandoned through physical, emotional, or sexual abuse.

Those responsible for us may have abandoned us by allowing the abuse to happen. Whatever the manner of abandonment we experienced, the pain is carried within us until it is healed.

Another premise of Inner Child healing work is that our childhood pain can only be healed through love. As adults, the only form of love that can heal the pain is self-love. To love ourselves we must release fear and old negative beliefs that are based on the pain of our childhood wounds. In order to do that, we must allow ourselves to fully grieve for those wounds. In order to grieve, we need to fully feel and acknowledge the pain. Only then can we fully express the pain and finally release it.

Many people believe that we should simply remove the past from our minds, pick ourselves up, and move on with life. However, just picking ourselves up and moving on with life never works. The danger with the "let's just move on" philosophy is that the pain can come out in destructive ways when not felt and acknowledged for what it is.

The main function of Inner Child work is to take responsibility for our own feelings and for our own lives; it is not to place blame on others. The purpose of expressing our anger and our hurt is to release it. In Inner Child work, we actually forgive those who have harmed us and create the space to feel compassion for them and for ourselves.

The first part of Inner Child healing is to meet and connect with the child part of our personality. This is done through visualization, drawing, speaking, or writing. Meeting the child within is crucial to healing because it is the first big step toward helping the child trust us enough to express the pain within.

> *To love ourselves we must release*
> *fear and old negative beliefs*
> *that are based on the pain of our*
> *childhood wounds.*

I teach people to begin connecting with their Inner Child by allowing the child to draw a picture of themselves. Then I invite them to have a conversation with their Inner Child in writing. I have them begin by writing a few simple sentences to the child. They write their (adult) part with the dominant hand and allow the child to answer with the non-dominant hand. Using the non-dominant hand allows the person to access their right brain, which is the intuitive area of thought.

The next part of Inner Child healing is to help the child fully feel and acknowledge their pain. This second step is also done through visualizing, writing, drawing, and speaking. I use guided visualizations and writing to help people get in touch with their Inner Child's pain. I teach them to begin talking and listening to the child, allowing the child to express their pain in words.

Janet is a client who worked with me to learn to heal her Inner Child. She continues that healing work on her own today. Below is a sample of her first writing to her child. It is similar to many clients' beginning writing to their Inner Child:

Adult: Hello, Little Janet. How old are you today? (This is important because the child will be different ages at different times, depending on the pain to be healed.)

Child: Nine months.

Adult: I am here to get to know you better. Would you draw me a picture of yourself so that I can see you more? (The person draws a picture of their Inner Child with their non-dominant hand).

Adult: Thank you very much for the picture! Now I can see you better. Is there anything you need from me today?

Child: Hold me.

Adult: I will hold you right now (The adult then actually puts her physical arms out to hold the child). I love you very much and want to get to know you more and more. I will talk to you again tomorrow.

When Janet did daily writing to her Inner Child, she found out that her child was very angry for all the abuse she had received from her mother, and she was very angry with Janet for not being there for her now. Janet kept talking and listening to her Inner Child through writing until the child was ready to fully express the pain that had been there for most of her life.

As pain is fully felt, acknowledged, and expressed, it releases in chunks. I use the word *chunks* because the process of releasing pain is actually experienced in that way. One thought or memory comes up with a wave of emotion. It moves through the body and out. But then another one comes up— either soon after the first or at an entirely different time when working with the Inner Child. That thought or memory moves through the body and out. The negative thoughts or memories that move through the body are chunks of negative energy that have been stored there. We can feel the negative energy as tightness, stress, or physical pain, and it can lead to chronic physical pain or illness.

As the old negative energy is released, something needs to fill the space where it was once held. If left empty, there can be a tendency to fill the space by pulling negative energy back in. What is needed to fill the space is love energy, and one way we can give loving energy to our Inner Child is through unconditional nurturing.

We can discover what kind of nurturing our Inner Child needs by maintaining an ongoing dialogue with the child. At first Janet found that her Inner Child was about nine months old and just needed to be held. So she held her in her arms a lot and told her how much she loved her. She actually physically held her arms around herself visualizing that she was holding her Inner Child. As she continued her healing, the child began to stand up at times. Then Janet began to hold her on her lap.

Many of my clients have similar experiences. Their Inner Child asks to be nurtured by being held. Besides being held, many Inner Children like to be nurtured by having lullabies sung to them, by taking long bubble baths, and through hearing loving words spoken to them.

After Inner Children are nurtured by their adults, they often want to play. That is the next step in Inner Child healing, and it is often the most difficult one for many people. As the oldest child in a family of five siblings, Janet learned that her role was to parent others. She continued that role well into her adult life and did not allow herself enough time to play. However, this was not only because she was the oldest child. She never allowed herself enough playtime because her pain held her down.

I have found the same to be true with many of my clients. Their childhood pain causes depression or at least keeps them from allowing themselves to play. The Inner Child needs to fully grieve the pain, fully release the pain, and then receive unconditional nurturing and play.

Janet began the healing work with her Inner Child in her thirties, and her work has been an ongoing process. Even though she has completed most of her grieving and releasing of pain, she has found that unconditional nurturing and play are an ongoing challenge, ever evolving as she continues her journey.

The kind of nurturing that she gives herself today involves allowing herself time alone just to *be*, surrounded by plants and water in a special space she has created for herself in her home. She has also found that she needs food that gives her the greatest nourishment and has changed her diet to reflect that new awareness. The area of nurturing that she finds she needs to focus on now is getting enough sleep on a nightly basis. She has changed her work schedule, trusting herself to allow some tasks to be put off until another day.

It takes an immense amount of trust for Janet to give herself the nurturing she really needs. Because of her childhood abuse, she learned to believe that she was unworthy of love and nurturing. She learned to mistrust the affection and nurturing offered by others and she could never give it to herself. As she has been able to trust herself more, nurturing herself becomes easier. Healing her Inner Child has given Janet a much deeper trust of herself and everyone else.

Janet is also looking for more ways to create play in her life. Her play today involves time in nature, especially in the mountains and at the beach. She has always felt drawn to these spaces, and today she can finally give herself time to be surrounded by nature without guilt.

Before doing Inner Child healing, Janet was not able to stay at the beach alone for more than half an hour without feeling guilty. Playing alone was the hardest play for Janet to allow herself to have. Playing alone is essential for healing our Inner Child because it gives love to us in a very special way that cannot be a mask for codependence. There is no one else around to try to please or try to get love from.

The last step in Inner Child healing is expressing creativity. Little children are naturally creative. The Inner Child is the part of our personality that is closest to our unique spirit and is naturally creative. The child values feelings, play, imagining, creating, and loving.

Janet's creativity was stifled at many turns before beginning Inner Child work. She had many creative ideas that she could not bring to fruition. This was because she had difficulty playing, which is a prerequisite to creativity. Even though she was able to carry through on a good number of creative ideas—enough to satisfy the adult within her—the full freedom of creativity that she really wanted always seemed to be on just the other side of the rainbow. Today that freedom is beginning to blossom in her life.

The Inner Child needs to fully grieve pain, fully release pain, and then receive unconditional nurturing and play.

It is essential in Inner Child healing to resolve and complete any "unfinished business" we may have with anyone, even if those persons are no longer living on earth. To do this I use a powerful visualization process to complete whatever needs to be healed in any relationship. I use the visualization especially for healing relationships with those persons who were involved in my clients' painful childhood experiences. However, it is also very helpful to use in healing any relationship in which the Inner Child still experiences pain.

I first ask the client to write a letter to the person with whom they have "unfinished business." In the letter they express the feelings that are not yet completed. Then I have them visualize the person with whom they have "unfinished business" sitting across from them. I ask them to read the letter out loud to the person, expressing the feelings in the letter and any other feelings that they still need to express. The time this takes is dependent on the particular circumstances or issues to be resolved.

Once the client has verbalized everything, I ask them to express silently that they are now ready to let go of the negative feelings they have held toward this person. I then invite them to tell the person anything they appreciate about them. Completing this "unfinished business" and giving voice to unexpressed emotion is a difficult thing to do. But to do so and to then be able to acknowledge one's willingness and intent to fully release the old feelings is a very healing experience.

> *Visualization can help us heal relationships*
> *with people who were involved in our*
> *painful childhood experiences.*

Kevin was a client in his forties who came to me because his childhood pain with his father was surfacing in his marriage relationship and in his work life. Throughout his 20s and 30s, he had kept down the pain of his physical and emotional abuse through drinking and overworking.

He married in his late thirties, and by the time he was forty he found that his drinking was a threat to both his marriage and his career. He stopped drinking and attended Alcoholics Anonymous meetings two times a week.

Things slowly improved in his home and work life, but then the anger that had been submerged came rushing to the surface. Kevin found himself very angry with everyone in his life. He lost his temper with his wife, his boss, and his co-workers almost daily. It was at this point that Kevin came to me and told me about his childhood abuse. When he felt ready, we began doing Inner Child healing work in which he was able to access the feelings of anger, fear, and hopelessness he had held inside for many years. I used the "unfinished business" visualization with him when he was ready to express these feelings to his father.

Kevin had written a letter to his father the day before he came to see me. The letter gave him a structure for what he wanted and needed to say after so many years of keeping it inside. I told him to first visualize his father however he looked to him at that moment. He visualized his father as a young man in his thirties, the age that his father was when Kevin was a young boy. He described him to me in enough detail so that he could feel his father in the visualization.

Kevin then began reading the letter. At first he did not show much emotion, but as he continued he sounded more and more angry. Toward the end of the letter, he began feeling the fear and hopelessness he had carried within for so many years.

He expressed to his father the deep anger he felt toward him for having to feel afraid and to keep the fear inside for so long. During the second part of the visualization, Kevin felt a release of some of the anger. We talked at the end of the session about that release and decided to do another visualization during our next session.

During the time he was in therapy with me, Kevin did several "unfinished business" visualizations with his father, which greatly enhanced the other aspects of Inner Child healing he was doing. He also did several visualizations with other significant people in his life with whom he had also harbored anger for many years. Today he has found peace in his daily life in all his relationships, and he continues to do Inner Child healing on his own.

"Unfinished business" visualizations sometimes lead a client to speak with the actual person. Kevin was able to speak with his father in person about a year after his initial visualization experience. Kevin told his father about the healing he was doing in his life. He spoke of the anger that he still felt about some incidents in the past. His father was actually able to listen for a short period of time. That was enough for Kevin. Speaking his truth to his own father helped him move forward a great deal on his healing journey.

An important aspect of "unfinished business" visualizations, however, is that it is not necessary to speak with the actual person in order to heal the old pain. It is the direct energetic expression of the pain that does the healing. Many of my clients use the visualization experiences to heal old pain with people who are deceased or with people they may never speak to again in person. Their experiences have been just as complete as those who actually speak in person or have an ongoing relationship with the person in everyday life.

Inner Child healing helps us access
and release feelings of anger,
fear, and hopelessness we have held
inside for many years.

One way to begin Inner Child healing on your own is to do the meditation at the end of this chapter. Some people more easily connect with their Inner Child in such a meditation. Others find that the writing method I have described here fits them better. If you are interested in doing the "unfinished business" visualization, I strongly suggest that you find a professional healer to do that work with you. It is most effective when experienced with a person who serves as a knowledgeable guide who can interact with you during the process.

Connecting with your Inner Child is one of the most powerful healing experiences you can have in this lifetime. Healing the child part of your personality enables you to feel a deep inner connection with yourself. That connection allows you to live in the present moment and brings natural peace and joy as you walk your spiritual journey on this earth. It can open creative and loving possibilities for you in this lifetime that you never thought were possible.

FOR REFLECTION

1. Make a greeting card note for your Inner Child. Sit with the note in quiet reflection for a few minutes. How do you feel?

2. What kind of pain do you feel in your life? Anger? Sadness? Disappointment? Fear? Does it seem that any of that pain is coming from the past?

3. Reflect on your daily life. Do you feel present in your life each day? What are two changes you could make at this time to help you feel more present?

MEDITATION
CONNECTING WITH YOUR INNER CHILD

1. Choose a quiet room or location where you will not be interrupted. Sit or lie in a comfortable position and close your eyes. Breathe deeply for a few moments. Notice any pain or tension anywhere in your body. Gently breathe into those tense parts of your body, breathing out the tension and pain.

2. Imagine yourself in a beautiful place—a place you've been before or a new place you create now. Walk around your beautiful place and experience what you see, hear, and smell there. Just be in your place of beauty for a few moments.

3. Whenever you are ready, imagine your Inner Child standing in front of you. What does your Inner Child look like? What is your Inner Child wearing? Spend a few moments just being with this child.

4. Now begin a conversation with your child, asking how old they are and how they are feeling today. Respond to your child and tell them that you want to get to know them better. Ask what they need from you right now. Respond truthfully, letting your child know what you will do in order to give them what they need.

5. Finish your conversation by telling your child you want to talk and listen and learn to love them more. Tell your child good bye.

6. Feel yourself slowly coming back to present time, knowing you can talk and listen to your child in this way at any time you wish. Feel yourself back in the room. Feel your feet and legs, your arms and hands. Feel yourself in present time now, ready to take care of that little child.

CHAPTER TWO

HEALING THROUGH RELATIONSHIPS

Many of us have chosen to live together with significant others, such as spouses and partners. Some of us have children or others that we guide as they grow. All of us have mothers and fathers, and many of us have siblings and extended families. Even if we live alone, we have interactions and relationships with a great number of human beings. All of us yearn for love and for loving relationships. Relationships are tremendously powerful healing forces in our lives. They create the daily interactions with other human beings that can teach us that we are not alone. They can remind us that we are beautiful and powerful beings bound together in one purpose on earth.

All loving relationships are rooted in an exchange of positive energy. This positive energy, which is often called Universal Life Force Energy, is exchanged when any being sees the beauty in another being. The more each being allows itself to be seen, the greater the energy flow.

This energy exchange does not only happen with human beings. It occurs between all beings in our universe. All beings contain within themselves an energy flow through which they grow and live with other beings on the earth. When we see the beauty within a plant, for example, we send a positive flow of energy to the plant. The plant receives the energy and sends energy to us in return. The same thing happens when we see the beauty in other earth beings, such as oceans and rivers or in stars or other planets in our solar system.

As human beings, many of us first learn to experience this positive energy with other human beings. When our parents or other caregivers see our beauty, they send us positive energy, which begins an interactive flow of energy between us. As we grow, we interact with other human beings who see our beauty and we see theirs. Through this positive energy exchange, we can heal the old pain of feeling separated from others.

The feeling of separation isn't something that we are only struggling with at this moment in time. It is something that human beings have struggled with for eons. This fear of separateness became part of the human story millennia ago when our connectedness to God, or Divine Source, was forgotten. We forgot that we are all a part of Divine Source, each expressing the energy of Divine Source in our own way. And we forgot our connectedness to the universe, to the earth, to each other, and to ourselves.

Master Kuthumi says: *Human relationships are created by you to learn the lessons of connection that you need to learn as you evolve on planet Terra (earth). You learn and grow in relationships with others in five main ways: by finishing karma, by healing old shadow pain, by learning through teaching, by merging, and by companionship. As you move on your paths of experience wherever you live, people will walk into your lives who can relate to you in all of these ways. They are your teachers as you are theirs. Receive into your hearts the lessons they bring you and accept humbly that you also teach them.*

If you are able to receive when it is time and give when it is time, you will move quickly on your paths of evolving in this lifetime. And it is important to move more quickly now in order to move into higher consciousness with your planet. Time has speeded up and so you must speed up your spiritual lessons.

The greatest spiritual lesson that each of you must learn is the lesson of love. Through all of your relationships, you will finally learn to deeply and unconditionally love yourself and others. Relationships have been given to you to help you do that in a natural and grace-filled manner. Receive them when it is time. Allow them to be with you and heal you when it is time. Release them when it is time. And when you release them, they will move back into the web of life from which they came. They are gifts that you have created among you, and gifts they will remain as you move into higher consciousness on your amazing journey.

We are spiritual beings who have come to earth to experience life in third dimension, and healing in this dimension involves learning the lessons of connection.

Before we came to the earth, we made agreements with people we have related with in other lifetimes. We agreed to come together to finish our karma, to heal old pain, to teach each other, to merge with each other, and to be companions for each other.

Karma is a universal system of learning that can help us evolve as spiritual beings. Through karma we magnetize experiences into our lives in which we can heal our actions from past lifetimes that have caused harm to others and to ourselves. We also magnetize experiences through which we can release the negativity that we carry from the harm others have done to us.

One way we can heal and grow in relationships is by changing our past actions with the same beings we created them with in the first place. Sometimes we choose this way to finish our karma because it is directly related to our past experiences with those beings. At other times, we choose to heal our past actions with new players if it is more appropriate in the overall scheme of our lives. Most of us use both ways to heal and grow in relationships by finishing karma.

All loving relationships are rooted in an exchange of positive energy.

Joseph was a young man whose mother had died when he was five years old. He lived alone with his father the rest of his childhood and had been physically and emotionally abused during that time. He left home at the age of 18 to join the Army and to get away from his father. During the entire time he was in the Army, he had very little contact with his father. After completing his time with the Army, Joseph began working and decided that there was no reason to have any further contact with his father.

At the end of the first year in his new job, Joseph's immediate supervisor was promoted and a new supervisor was hired. The new boss reminded him of his father in many ways. The new boss not only had many similar personality traits as his father, but he even looked like his father. The worst part was that the new supervisor was verbally abusive. Joseph wanted to quit his job but felt he needed to stay at least another year for experience. He felt stuck just as he had with his father, and as the weeks went by, he became more and more depressed.

Joseph came to me feeling hopeless. After a few introductory sessions, we began with Inner Child healing. During that work Joseph saw a past lifetime he had experienced with his father. His father had actually been his brother in that lifetime and was extremely jealous of him. When Joseph became engaged to a young woman the brother was also interested in, he followed Joseph one night and physically attacked him. Joseph was seriously injured and never fully recovered from his wounds in that lifetime.

After having this particular lifetime revealed to him, Joseph came to understand that both he and his brother decided to come back together in this lifetime to heal the karma they both carried from that past relationship. Since we often come back to heal past wounds with the same people, many of the people we struggle with in the present may be people we need to complete karma with from the past.

I next began doing Belief/Fear Release work with Joseph in addition to Inner Child healing. In Belief/Fear Release work, I help people release self-defeating beliefs and fears that they bring from other lifetimes to heal. One of the beliefs that Joseph carried from the lifetime with his father was: "I will never be free from hatred and abuse." Joseph decided that he wanted to release that old belief and heal his side of the karma with his father.

After he released that belief, Joseph was able to take charge of his life in a new way. He began dealing with his supervisor in an assertive manner, and the verbal abuse lessened immediately. Within a few months the supervisor was moved to a new location, and Joseph began practicing the same assertiveness in all his relationships.

Six months later Joseph decided that he wanted to deal with his father in the same assertive manner. He realized that in order to heal the karma he needed to at least be able to speak to his father without accepting any abuse from him. He called his father and arranged to visit him.

Joseph spoke with his father about the past abuse and expressed his feelings to him. His father listened and expressed regret for what he had done. In the same conversation, however, Joseph's father became verbally abusive, so Joseph assertively told him that he would never accept abuse from him again. The visit ended in a strained manner, but since that time his father has called a number of times, talking to Joseph in a non-abusive manner. Joseph thinks his father is trying to make amends in the best way he knows how at this time, but whether or not his father ever completes his side of the healing, Joseph feels he has completed his side of the karma.

*Many of the people
we struggle with in the present may be people
we need to complete karma with
from the past.*

The second way Master Kuthumi indicated that we can grow in relationship with others is by healing our old shadow pain. Our "shadow self" is a part of ourselves that exists in the unconscious mind. It is made up of those parts of ourselves that we believe are unacceptable. We keep them hidden from ourselves because it is too painful to acknowledge them. Instead, we often see them in other people and blame others for possessing those same characteristics. If we are open to growing in relationship with others, we can work through our denial about these unwanted parts of ourselves. We can begin to heal our shadow pain by making it conscious, acknowledging it, and releasing it through our interactions. We can come to accept ourselves as we really are.

Dottie was a woman in her 40s whose husband died of a sudden heart attack at the age of 48. After an initial period of support from friends and family, she spent a lot of time alone with her deep grief. Her two daughters were away at college, and she refused invitations to spend time with friends. About a year after her husband's death, Dottie met a new co-worker who had also recently lost her husband. The co-worker convinced Dottie to accompany her to a grief support group.

As Dottie began to share in the group, she expressed feelings that she had kept hidden from herself for many years. Sparked by two members in the group who continually dominated the conversation, Dottie vocalized her anger at people who try to control others. The group responded to her in an open and compassionate manner. Slowly she began to feel safe in the group. She became more open to looking within herself as she interacted with the group over time. As she looked within herself, she began to recognize the way *she* had controlled others in her own life. Dottie had never seen this before. She had only noticed how other people were controlling and dominating. She had seen it in her mother and in one of her daughters. She had seen it in people at work.

Dottie's experience in the grief support group helped her access a part of her unconscious "shadow self" she considered unacceptable and therefore denied. She didn't allow herself to acknowledge this part of her because she was afraid that people would not love her if they saw this. But the support group provided the safety in which she could honestly look inside and see what needed to be healed. The group showed her respect and love as she learned and healed. Her blame of other people for controlling behavior diminished as she accepted those controlling parts of herself. Over the next year, she began to share more in her relationships with loved ones and found herself becoming less controlling in her daily life. Enjoyment became more important than control.

> *We can begin to heal our shadow pain*
> *by making it conscious,*
> *acknowledging it, and releasing it*
> *through our interactions.*

Learning by teaching is the next way that Master Kuthumi tells us that we can learn in relationships. We are all teachers of each other. The most obvious teaching relationships are those we take on as parents, leaders, or professional teachers in life. In these relationships our purpose is to guide and teach others to become who they really are, to help them actualize their special gifts as humans on unique spiritual paths. We teach them by listening, by speaking, and by modeling. Modeling means that they can watch us as we become who we truly are by using our own unique gifts to actualize ourselves as spiritual beings in the world.

Our children, students, and those we lead also come to teach us. They come to teach us to live in harmlessness and connectedness with ourselves and with all beings. They come to teach us to choose right action in our daily lives and to create a world where sharing and love reign.

Lupe and Tony were a couple in their early thirties who, because they could not have children of their own, decided to adopt a child from another country. Francesca came to live with them when she was three years old. They felt prepared to help her adjust to a completely different living environment, and they knew that she came with wounds that were explained to them by the adoption agency. They wanted to love Francesca and guide her to love herself. They wanted to help her release any pain she carried from her past and provide a safe haven for her to thrive and grow.

Lupe and Tony attended parenting classes before Francesca arrived, and both were in individual psychotherapy to heal any remaining childhood pain within themselves. They both felt good about their preparation for becoming parents, and when Francesca arrived they were indeed able to provide the safe haven they had wanted to give her. She thrived and grew within the loving structure they built for her.

What Lupe and Tony were not prepared for was all that Francesca would teach them. At four years of age, she began creating plays and enacting them with her preschool friends. Lupe and Tony were invited to attend the performances which took place in the family room.

Several of the plays featured reenacted interactions between Lupe and Tony themselves. As they watched

Francesca and her friends tell the stories, Lupe and Tony realized that these plays were displaying how they were still living with childhood pain. They saw how they were still expressing old pain in their daily interactions with each other.

In one of Francesca's plays, she showed an incident that had just taken place between Lupe and Tony a week before. In the play, Francesca reenacted a night when Lupe came home from work acting irritated and impatient. Tony felt hurt and took her behavior personally. He responded to anything Lupe said with silence. Lupe became more impatient and irritated with Tony for feeling hurt.

What Lupe did not tell Tony when she came home that night was that she was very angry with her employer for the harsh restrictions and rules he had announced that day. In her childhood, she was taught that anger was not an acceptable emotion, and she still had difficulty showing that emotion. As angry as she was with her employer, she did not want to show that anger at home, so she did not share with Tony what happened at work.

As they watched Francesca's play, Lupe and Tony realized that the incident was one of many in which neither of them could easily talk about their anger. Both had grown up with a "Don't be angry" rule and had carried that into adult life. The play nudged them to begin talking with each other about their anger and other emotions that were not acceptable in their families growing up.

Through this play and others, Lupe and Tony began to understand more deeply that they could begin to release old childhood pain through the intimacy of their relationship. They could find acceptance in telling each other their innermost feelings. They had provided a safe and loving family in which Francesca could heal her own early-childhood pain, but they never imagined that their daughter would help them heal from theirs. Their daughter was indeed a significant teacher in their lives.

We are all teachers of each other.

Merging is the next way that Master Kuthumi shows us that we can heal and grow in relationships. Merging is a spiritual combining of the gifts each of us brings to an intimate relationship as we deeply share ourselves through honest interaction. We came to this earth in order to learn through experience in relationship. All relationships lead back to oneness, to becoming intimate with all life. Merging in our most intimate relationships can be one of the most powerful and quickest ways back to oneness. Through merging, we experience, in a dramatic way, that we are each part of the other and ultimately part of the whole.

As we learn to merge with another, we feel the energy of deep connectedness which counteracts our feelings of separateness and fear. That deep connectedness, or intimacy, is shared in four ways. In *intellectual intimacy,* we share our innermost thoughts, ideas, and interests. In *emotional intimacy,* we share our innermost feelings. *Physical intimacy* is shared through close physical affection and sexual love. And *spiritual intimacy* is a sharing of our deepest values in life.

John and Elaine came to me for therapy because they were having difficulty sharing their innermost feelings, and this lack of deep communication was causing problems in their sexual relationship. They were not able to share either the depth of their love for each other or the hesitancies each had because of old childhood pain.

As I worked with John and Elaine for a period of a year, they practiced honest interaction both in my office and in the homework assignments they received from me each week. At first the homework assignments focused on intellectual intimacy because they were already good at sharing their thoughts, ideas, and interests. I encouraged them to practice forming an even deeper bond in this area by pursuing more interests together. They went camping in the mountains, which is something they had always wanted to do but had not made time for in their busy lives. I had them consciously practice slowing down in their daily lives, letting go of any unnecessary activities they did not love doing. They reduced errands to a bare minimum. They streamlined their responsibilities at home and their activities connected with work. Having fun together became a highlight in their lives.

As John and Elaine shared more intellectual intimacy and had more fun together, their emotional intimacy slowly increased in a natural way. During a camping trip, for example, they talked long into the night about their childhoods, including the abuse each had experienced. They had been reluctant to share that pain with each other until that moment.

In sharing their feelings that night, John and Elaine were able to see more deeply each other's inner beauty. As they saw that beauty more clearly, the energy of love was released between them. It was a breakthrough for their relationship, and they found deeper sexual intimacy in the following weeks.

I encouraged John and Elaine to practice sharing deeper feelings with each other in my office, and over a period of weeks they were able to continue the sharing that they had begun on the camping trip. They realized that much of their old pain was similar. They both had learned not to talk about their abuse for different reasons.

John's father was a severe disciplinarian who beat John for not following stringent rules. John was also beaten if he expressed any thoughts or feelings about the rules. If he talked about the beatings he received, he would be beaten again. Elaine was sexually abused by her stepfather, and when she told her mother about it, she was forbidden to ever speak about it again. Her mother convinced her that if she spoke about it, she would be responsible for sending her stepfather to jail. Both John and Elaine had learned in childhood not to talk about any deep feelings, whether positive or negative.

Speaking openly with each other allowed intimacy to grow through understanding and compassion. This ultimately

allowed John and Elaine to verbalize the deep love they had
for each other. At first they were both afraid that they would
lose the love they felt if they shared their feelings. They
experienced tremendous fear as they kept sharing, but it slowly
subsided as they merged both emotionally and physically
through honest interaction.

Verbalizing their deep love for each other also led John
and Elaine to begin sharing their deepest values in life.
They found that they had many deep values in common that
they had never shared before. Their spiritual intimacy grew,
and their love deepened.

Today John and Elaine continue to share their innermost
feelings, whether they are painful or positive, and their
merging has blossomed in a way they still find amazing.
A community of friends and family members has formed
around them who want to share in their positive, connecting
energy. All of these people are also evolving in sharing their
innermost feelings and appreciating the inner beauty of each
other. The merging of John and Elaine has extended outward
to many others through honest interaction.

All relationships lead back
to oneness, to becoming intimate
with all life.

The last way Master Kuthumi mentions that we can heal
and grow in relationships is through companionship. Long
before we came to this earth we lived together in spiritual

connection with Divine Source. On earth we are meant to be companions to one another to remember that oneness. We are meant to recognize that each person we meet has a message for us and we have a message for them. As we learn this truth, we can create truly conscious relationships with everyone in our lives.

Ariana was at the end of her first year of a master's program in international relations when she was offered an internship in a third-world country. She accepted the invitation with great enthusiasm. She knew that it supported her dream of getting to know, understand, and interact with people in different cultures and countries.

On weekends during the year of her internship, Ariana began traveling to nearby villages with two other interns, Peter and Colette. The three young interns were very interested in getting to know the local people and their way of life. The interns became traveling and connecting companions. Ariana enjoyed being with Peter and Colette very much because, although they came from Europe and she came from the United States, they were kindred spirits with similar interests and dreams for the future.

Ariana had other wonderful experiences of companionship with people in the villages she visited. On one trip, she met an older woman in the marketplace who was selling jewelry. The two began talking when they both realized that each knew something of the other's language. The woman, who was called Ruth, invited Ariana to come to her home on

Ariana's next trip to the village.

A month later Ariana and her two companions went to the village for a day, and Ariana introduced the interns to her new friend from the marketplace. The woman invited all three young people to her home for a late afternoon meal. It was the beginning of a bonding between the three "outsiders" and Ruth's entire family. Ruth lived with her mother, one of her married daughters, the daughter's husband, and their three children. Some of the family spoke more English than others, but no one seemed to have any problem with that. Conversations were lively and everyone was interested in hearing what everyone else had to say.

During the rest of the year, Ariana and her two companions visited the family as often as they could. Ariana felt like the family's home was her own home. She spent some time learning jewelry making from Ruth, and she and Ruth cooked together, sharing favorite recipes they each loved to create. Ariana felt a connection with Ruth that went deep into her soul.

Ariana had another experience of companionship that was very important to her during her internship. She met a young woman her own age in one of the other villages she visited for a particular work project. The woman's name was Karina, and she had been assigned to the project as a local representative. Karina spoke English fluently, and she had studied in the United States the previous year. The two young women quickly became friends.

During the time Ariana and Karina worked together, they were able to complete their tasks for the project more easily and quickly than anyone expected. They had fun working together and enjoyed creating ways to improve life for people in that country through their project. In the time that they worked on the project, the two friends also shared with each other their hopes and dreams for the future and the struggles they had experienced in their lives. They were not able to spend much time with each other outside of work, but they made plans to meet once their project was completed.

Ariana discovered that Karina was a companion who had very similar dreams and deep inner values as her own. She felt deeply affirmed in her desire to learn more about the interconnectedness of all people. She felt that interconnectedness, not only in her relationships with Ruth and Karina, but also in her relationships with her companion interns and with Ruth's family members. After her companion experiences with people during that special year of her life, Ariana knew that she had always sought that oneness with people in her heart, and that is why she had wanted to get to know the local people of that country.

We are meant to recognize
that each person we meet
has a message for us,
and we have a message for them.

As we see beauty in other beings and allow them to see beauty in us, a positive energy flow is created between us. That energy flow, which is Universal Life Force Energy, is the most healing energy in the world. It heals the fear of separateness that we took on so long ago when we began feeling disconnected from Divine Source, from our universe, the earth, and all other beings.

Joseph was finally able to see his own inner beauty as he spoke assertively to his father. Dottie exchanged positive energy with her support group as they saw her inner beauty and showed respect for her. Lupe and Tony connected intimately with each other as they learned from Francesca and discovered both their own and their daughter's tremendous beauty. John and Elaine saw each other's deep beauty as they shared their feelings on the camping trip and as they extended their connecting energy to many others in community. Ariana exchanged the positive energy of oneness as she built companionship with the other interns, with Ruth and her family, and with Karina during that important year of her life.

Relationships are amazing gifts that we have created and developed to remind us that we are all spiritually connected, that each of us is intimately needed and intertwined with the whole. Through all of our relationships, we will finally learn to deeply and unconditionally love ourselves and others. As Master Kuthumi reminds us, that is the greatest lesson we each must learn.

For Reflection

1. Do you have someone in your life at this time with whom you feel you need to finish karma? What is your next step to do the healing you need to do with that person?

2. Do you find yourself blaming others for characteristics you see in them? Allow yourself to look at one of those characteristics to see if it might be part of your old shadow pain.

3. Are you learning by teaching anyone in your life at this time? What are you learning from that person?

4. Are you learning and growing in relationship through merging with someone at this time? What is your next step in that process?

MEDITATION
CONNECTING WITH YOUR COMPANIONS

The following meditation can help you feel the energy of companionship and connectedness with all of the people in your everyday life.

1. Close your eyes and take a few deep breaths...notice your breathing as you breathe in and breathe out...notice any pain or tension anywhere in your body...gradually breathe into those tense parts, breathing out the tension...feel yourself letting go.

2. Imagine you are going inward toward the center of your being...deeper and deeper...inward...inward into the center of your heart...see a beautiful pink crystal ball of light shining within your heart...stay with that wondrous crystal light for the next few moments.

3. Now imagine beautiful sparkling rays of that pink crystal light streaming out from your heart to the hearts of each person in your everyday life...see each person in the different areas of your life...your immediate family...your friends...your work companions...see yourself sending love energy to each one of these people you accompany on your daily journey in life.

4. See yourself walking up to some of your life companions...join hands with them and continue sending the sparkling rays of crystal light from your heart to

their hearts...see the beauty deep within them...feel your connection to them...feel the love within your heart for them...be there with them for a few moments, and as you leave them, know that you can bring those feelings of connection back to your everyday life.

5. Feel yourself coming back to present time...feel your body sitting or lying in the room where you are...feel your arms and your legs, your hands and your feet...feel yourself coming back to present time with feelings of love for the companions in your life...whenever you are ready, open your eyes, feeling clear and energized for the rest of your day.

CHAPTER THREE

HEALING THROUGH PAST LIVES

In order to fully feel our connection with ourselves and to feel oneness and peace with others, we need to heal our wounds from the past. Besides healing our childhood pain, we also need to heal the wounds from our past lifetimes. We all have other times that we have come to earth to live in the third dimension. During those lifetimes, we had many experiences as we evolved in learning the lessons of love that we all came to learn. During those experiences, there were times that we harmed others or ourselves or were harmed by others. The negative decisions we made at those times became the wounds of karma that we carried with us to heal in future lifetimes.

Any karma we have not healed in our past lives we bring for healing to our present lifetime. That healing comes when we release the negative energy within, allowing the positive energy of love to flow through us unimpeded by those past decisions. It is that positive love energy flowing through us that takes us into the higher consciousness of deep connectedness and sharing.

I asked Lord Maitreya about the importance of healing karma in order to ascend with the earth. He answered: *It is very important to release past-life karma today in order to ascend to the higher dimensions with the earth. Humans must learn the lessons of sharing and unity today. In your past lives, many of you were far from those concepts, and many are still today. Past life karma is the result of harming yourselves and others while on your evolutionary paths. The harm you have done is carried within until it is healed and released. All negativity from the harm others have done to you must also be released. Then the Divine light of higher consciousness can dwell brightly within each human. The Divine spark is always there, but it must be greatly enhanced today in order to live on an earth of unity, love, and peace. As you help others to release karma, you will be purifying yourself as well. So too will it be with each worker of light on your earth. Each person who brings healing to others will assist many to choose sharing instead of greed and unity instead of separatism. By helping others, each worker of light will also release any greed and separatism that they still carry within. They will purify their own hearts. Releasing all past-life karma is essential to the spiritual leaps that must be made by all persons who want to move into higher consciousness with the earth.*

The wounds of karma cause feelings of separateness and deep pain. Those feelings come from the negative decisions we make as we harm others or ourselves. They also come when we are harmed by others in daily life. Those negative decisions become the fears and limiting beliefs that we carry from lifetime to lifetime until they are released and the karma is healed. For example, in a lifetime in which someone harms another through abandonment, the person abandoned might decide "I'll never stay with anyone again." The fear that comes from that decision could be "I'm afraid that someone will leave me," and a limiting belief that they carry to their next lifetimes could easily be "People always go away."

Karma keeps us from being free to fully live in our present lives because we live in the past that we drag around with us. We cannot fall into place in our daily lives. We can heal karma through relationships with our Inner Child and with other human beings in this lifetime. We can also heal karma by consciously connecting with the pain from other lifetimes in which the negative decisions were made and the harm was done. As we consciously connect with and acknowledge the wounds from those lifetimes, the pain can move through our body and release.

Connecting consciously with the pain of our past lives can happen in a number of ways. We can spontaneously see scenes from other lives which usually come when we are in a meditative state or asleep. We can do regression work with a therapist who helps us see incidents in the past in which we have experienced certain negative feelings that we also experience in this lifetime. We can also do Belief/Fear Release work in which we heal the pain from past lives without necessarily seeing or recalling those lifetimes.

Karma keeps us from being free to fully live in our present lives because we live in the past that we drag around with us.

I have found Belief/Fear Release to be the method that is most helpful for my clients to heal the wounds of karma. Since the negative decisions we made became the limiting beliefs and fears that we carry within, dealing directly with those beliefs and fears seems to work most quickly and easily with most people. By allowing the beliefs or fears to rise up and move through the body and be released, many people can come to a healing experience that is truly transformational. Since the beliefs and fears are usually connected to intense emotional energy stored in the body, the release work allows that energy to leave the body as the pain is transformed into love.

The process I use for Belief/Fear Release work is a very simple yet powerful one. I first help the person explore their thoughts to get the actual words of the subconscious limiting belief or fear. It usually comes as the person talks about the emotional pain they are feeling. The words may be something like "People never stay with me" or "I'm afraid that I will never have love in my life" or even "If I do the work I love, I will die." It may take some time to get the actual words of the belief or fear if it has been buried in the subconscious over a lifetime or many lifetimes. As people get used to finding their limiting beliefs and fears, however, those beliefs and fears come to the surface more quickly.

Once someone has the words of the belief or fear, it is written down. Then I guide them into a meditative state and ask them to see a picture in the front of their mind that goes along with the belief or fear. When they have the picture, I ask them to "freeze" it and put it aside for the moment. They will come back to it later. Then I ask them to "go into their body" and feel any physical sensations that seem to be connected to the picture. They report where those feelings are in their body. The sensations are usually ones of constriction in certain areas where negative energy is stored.

I next ask them to begin breathing into those areas with cleansing breaths. The person breathes in through their nose into the areas they have mentioned and out through their mouth. I ask them to continue the breathing until the physical sensations are gone from their body. Throughout this process, I assist them in releasing the feelings by sending them healing energy while they are breathing.

When the person tells me that the physical sensations are gone from their body, I ask them to bring the picture back to the front of their mind. They then destroy the picture in their mind's eye in a manner of their choice. They may burn it, blow it up, or shred it and burn the pieces. Once the picture is destroyed, I help the person think of an affirmation to say every day in order to keep the limiting belief or fear from coming back into the body. An affirmation is a positive statement that goes against negative statements that we tell ourselves. It helps to integrate the healing the person has just received. An example of an affirmation for the belief "People never stay with me" is "I live in relationships with security and ease." For the belief "If I do the work I love I will die," an affirmation could be "Doing the work I love is life-giving and life-enhancing." For the fear "I'm afraid that I will never have love in my life," a good affirmation might be "I feel love in every part of my life. I give and receive love every day of my life."

After a Belief/Fear Release session, most people are so open to positive spiritual energy that affirmations come easily to mind. I ask the client to say the affirmation every day and say it even more when the old belief or fear tries to find its way back into the mind and body. The positive energy of the affirmation keeps love energy flowing freely inside the person, taking the place of the negative energy of the belief or fear.

By allowing beliefs or fears to rise up and move through the body and be released, many people can come to a healing experience that is truly transformational.

Lena came to me because she felt her life was not working in any area. Her marriage of ten years was over. One morning her husband told her that he no longer loved her and left that night. They had been having problems in their relationship for some time before that night, but Lena never thought the issues between them would lead to a breakup.

Soon after Lena's husband left, her work position was eliminated. She knew there were financial problems in the company, and she knew that other positions had been eliminated because of cutbacks. But she never thought that her position would be eliminated because it was so crucial to the company's success.

A few days after Lena had been laid off at work, her daughter Joanna called her in tears, saying that her husband had become violent and hit her several times. Joanna had decided to leave him and needed to stay with Lena for a short time. When Lena came to see me, her daughter and three grandchildren had been with her for two months. Lena was trying to look for a new job, but some days she could not get out of the house at all due to her own depression and her daughter's needs.

Once Lena was able to work through some practical issues in her daily life, we began looking at the subconscious limiting beliefs that she carried within. Over the next few months, we uncovered many beliefs that kept her from feeling and using her full power to create her life. Some of those beliefs included "If I don't look at things, nothing bad will happen to me," "Other people are more important than I am. If I take care of them, I will be taken care of," and "I don't have what it takes to move ahead on my own."

I began to use Belief/Fear Release work with Lena for these three beliefs, and one of her past lives became known. As is true for most of us, Lena was with someone in that lifetime that she again knows in her present lifetime. Many people we know in this lifetime can be people from our past lives. We make agreements with them before we come into this lifetime to come back together to finish karma.

In that past lifetime, Lena was in an abusive relationship with the same man who had been her husband in this lifetime. He had supported her financially, so she stayed with him in that past lifetime until he almost killed her. At that point she ran for her life and ended up living on the streets with barely enough food to stay alive. The decision she made at that time was "I don't have what it takes to make it on my own." That decision became a limiting belief that she carried to her current lifetime in order to heal it and to know her true power as a spiritual human being. Lena was now ready to heal this belief and the others that had kept her from feeling that power during most of her life.

As we continued the healing work, Lena was able to set and maintain appropriate boundaries with her daughter, find work in which she could use her strong people skills, and begin new relationships with people in which she received as much as she gave.

Many people we know in this lifetime can be people from our past lives.

Ned came to me after he lost his job. He had lost three jobs in the last six years. All of the jobs were doing work he enjoyed. He was very successful in finding work he enjoyed and that paid very well. Things went well for about the first year in each position. After the first year, however, problems would arise for him with his supervisor or his co-workers. Everything seemed to go downhill after that. Incidents took place with co-workers in which he was blamed, and these incidents were recorded in his file. He had disagreements with his supervisors that led to verbal and written warnings. He would eventually be fired or laid off.

The reason Ned came to me for help was that he finally saw that he had lost all the jobs he wanted most in his life. He was only able to stay in positions in which he was not happy. As he told me the stories of his work life over the past twenty years, he got in touch with the limiting belief "I have to do work I hate or I'll starve." At that point, I began doing Belief/Fear Release work with him, using that belief and several others that came up during the next few months.

After doing several sessions of Belief/Fear Release work, it came to Ned that he had a number of lifetimes in which he did work that was demeaning or meaningless to him. During one session, he spontaneously saw a lifetime in which he was a slave doing demeaning work. He felt secure doing that work because the alternative was starvation. At one point in that lifetime, when he felt he would never be released from slavery, he made the decision that he would always have to do demeaning and meaningless work. He carried the karma of that negative decision into his future lifetimes as the belief "I have to do work I hate or I'll starve." During our session Ned realized that he brought that belief into his present lifetime to heal.

Through Belief/Fear Release work, Ned finally released the karma and its old pain from his mind and body. He began looking for work again, confident that he could find a position he loved and keep it. He also completed several classes he needed for his teaching credential. Today he is truly enjoying his work as a high school theater teacher and acting coach. He also does acting himself in a local community theater. He has all the money he needs to live comfortably. It is the fulfillment of a lifetime dream for his work in the world.

> *Belief/Fear Release*
> *work can help us*
> *release karma and its pain*
> *from our mind and body.*

It is not necessary to see or recall our past lifetimes in order to do Belief/Fear Release work. Since the healing is done at the emotional and physical levels, all that is needed is to bring to consciousness a limiting belief or fear that we want to release and then to move through the steps to release it. If that belief or fear comes from a negative decision we made in a past lifetime, the process can be used to heal the karma and pain from that lifetime, whether we are conscious of it or not.

One of the wonderful things about Belief/Fear Release work is that whatever a person needs to feel and release at that time comes up. They might need to feel a fear that has been carried throughout life. It could even be a fear they have worked on releasing many times during their entire adult life but have just come to the point when they can completely let it go. They might need to complete the karma from a past life in which they made a decision that became a limiting belief they could not release for many lifetimes. They could now be ready to fully feel and acknowledge the pain of that belief, and if they are willing to do the release work, they can finally let it go.

Whatever it is people need to feel and release, it will always free them to know more completely who they really are and help them feel their true power as spiritual human beings. The pain they have carried through many lifetimes will finally be transformed into love, and they can move into the higher consciousness of deep connectedness, unity, and peace.

FOR REFLECTION

1. Has any limiting belief come to your consciousness recently that you want to release at this time? How is that belief harming you in your present life?

2. Make a list of the fears that are keeping you from fully living your life at this time. Which ones do you feel ready to release?

MEDITATION
RELEASING FEAR

In the meditation that follows, choose a fear that you want to release from your life. Write it down in a sentence, such as "I am afraid that I cannot have the money I need in my life" or "I am afraid that I will disappoint the people I love."

1. Close your eyes and take a few deep breaths. Allow yourself to just be for the next few moments.

2. Think of the fear that you wish to release at this time. See a picture in the front of your mind that goes along with that fear.

3. Freeze that picture and put it aside. You will bring the picture back later.

4. Go into your body and notice any physical feelings that go along with the picture.

5. Begin breathing into those areas with deep, cleansing breaths (breathe in through your nose and out through your mouth). Keep breathing until the feelings are released. Take as much time as you need.

6. When the feelings in your body are released, bring the picture back to the front of your mind.

7. Destroy the picture by tearing it up and burning it, blowing it up, or destroying it in another way that feels right to you.

8. Once the picture is gone, allow an affirmation (positive statement) to come to you that you can say daily to help you integrate the release of this fear. For example, if the fear was "I am afraid that I will never have the money I need in my life," an affirmation might be "Money comes to me easily, and I have abundance in all areas of my life." Write the affirmation down.

9. Write or say your affirmation daily as you integrate this healing into your life. Use the affirmation especially when you are tempted to go back into the old fear.

10. If any pictures of past lives came to your consciousness while doing this meditation, journal about those pictures. If you have difficulty understanding what you have seen or difficulty releasing the fear, get help from a healer who works with past lives and fear release.

CHAPTER FOUR

CONNECTING WITH
SPIRITUAL LIGHT BEINGS

Conscious relationships with spiritual light beings can speed up our healing and feelings of connectedness within ourselves, with others, and with the entire universe. Some spiritual light beings are light beings who have never had a third-dimensional lifetime. Others have walked this earth but are now living in the spiritual light realms. Spiritual light beings include angels and archangels, Ascended Masters from our planet, and light beings from other parts of the universe. What all spiritual light beings have in common is that they live in the light realms of the higher dimensions.

There are 13 dimensions of existence connected to life on earth. The first dimension is the realm of the mineral kingdom. The second is the realm of bacteria and other simple life forms. The third dimension is the realm of all other beings on earth: plants, animals, and humans. The entire earth is now in the process of moving into the fourth dimension. Once that shift is complete, the first three dimensions will not be part of our earth experience.

The fourth dimension is the dimension of flow. Beings who live continually at this dimensional level have a body that in the past has been lighter than ours. Beings who live in this realm include fairies and loving nature guardians. We humans on earth have always participated in the fourth dimension in our feelings and dreams. Since our earth is now moving into the Age of Light, our bodies are also becoming lighter as we release the density of old pain and stuck energy. We are moving toward living in the flow of the fourth dimension in our daily lives.

The fifth dimension has an energy flow that is increased even more greatly than that of the fourth dimension. Many spiritual light beings, who are teachers and guides for humans, live continually in this realm. There are angels and Ascended Masters from our planet, but there are spiritual light beings from other solar systems and galaxies as well. The sixth dimension is the realm of geometric form, which is necessary for creation. It is also the realm of the Higher Self, the part of us that is always connected to the universe and who knows our higher purpose for being on earth at this time. The seventh dimension is the realm of Divine light through sound, and the eighth dimension is the realm of Divine light through color.

The ninth, tenth, eleventh, and twelfth dimensions move closer and closer to the state of oneness that exists at the thirteenth dimension. It is at this, the thirteenth-dimensional state of consciousness, that we no longer feel any kind of separation. We live in oneness with Divine Source.

Conscious relationships with spiritual light beings
can speed up our healing and feelings
of connectedness within ourselves,
with others, and with the entire universe.

Because our earth is now moving into the Age of Light, many Ascended Masters and other spiritual light beings have chosen to take on human bodies and come to earth to help us at this auspicious time. Some stay among us on earth to teach and guide us, and others take on human bodies for short periods of time when we have special need of their help. Many do not come to earth but have greatly increased their contact with us from the higher dimensions. All are offering assistance to us as we evolve toward living in the higher dimensions.

Angels have a very crucial role to play as we move into the Age of Light. They have always been there for us spiritually, helping us and guiding us even when we did not know they were there. Many individuals over the history of time on earth *did* know they were there. They asked for and received the assistance of angels in times of need. Angels even manifested physically when needed to bring important messages to those people. But now angels are making themselves known more openly to all of us when we are ready for their help. They communicate with us from the spiritual light realms and take on bodies whenever that is needed to get their messages across. They offer guidance, assistance, and encouragement for our spiritual growth and are always careful to honor our free will. They can help us release the feelings of separateness we carry from past pain. And since the specialty of angels is joy, communicating with them can help us release fear in our lives.

Ascended Masters from the earth have taken the journey into the higher dimensions before us. Many of them have chosen to assist humans on the earth to take that journey now. Those Ascended Masters who are actually living on earth at this time are able to bilocate and appear in many places at once if that is needed in order to do the spiritual work they have come to do. They understand our need to heal karma and our need to connect with our Higher Self in this lifetime. Our Higher Self is the part of us that is always connected to the universe and to Divine Source. The Ascended Masters offer us teaching, support, and encouragement as we move on our spiritual path.

There are three ways we can consciously connect with spiritual light beings. The first way is to spontaneously receive their messages, which can come in words, pictures, or feelings. This happens many times while we are in a meditative state, but it can happen at any time in daily life. The second way is to consciously write or speak to them and wait to hear their response, which can come in words, pictures, or feelings. As we write or speak to spiritual light beings and receive their messages, we can have an ongoing conversation and relationship with them. The third way to consciously connect with spiritual light beings is to spontaneously meet them in a bodily form. That meeting usually comes when they have a special message for us that we urgently need to hear at a certain time in our life.

Randy was a young man in his 30s who was working on healing his childhood pain. He attended several of my Inner Child classes and was learning to feel more connected to himself as he wrote daily to his Inner Child. He also began to journal and pray as part of his daily spiritual practice. As Randy was journaling one evening about the gratitude he felt for his inner healing, the words spontaneously came in his writing "I am your guardian angel and have always been with you in your daily life. I, too, am grateful for all the healing you are receiving in your life. I will help you in that healing. You have only to ask and I will respond to you in support and love."

Randy wrote back to his guardian angel "I am so grateful to have you in my life. I want to speak to you and get to know you better. I want to receive your help with my healing every day of my life. I will begin writing to you in my journaling time. Thank you for your love." He continued writing to his guardian angel each day and received guidance and support that helped him in the healing work he was doing with his Inner Child.

Angels offer guidance, assistance, and encouragement for our spiritual growth and are always careful to honor our free will.

In my early 40s, I was attracted to reading spiritual books that were channeled by spiritual light beings. The purpose of their messages was to guide us as humans to evolve into the higher dimensions. When I read books channeled from these beings, I felt very much that I had "come home." All of a sudden there were written words in front of me about things I had always known in my heart but had no arena in my life in which to freely express.

I did share that deep knowing at certain times of my life, but many responses I received only reinforced that I was "different" or "not good enough." For example, when I was a teenager, I shared in a religion class that love is the most important thing in the world. I was reprimanded for not understanding the whole truth. Because of this, I learned to be cautious about expressing the spiritual truths I knew deep down. So when I read about spiritual evolution and moving toward oneness and higher spiritual dimensions, it was wonderful and freeing.

After that time, I began connecting with spiritual light beings who became my teachers and guides, and journaling became my favorite way to connect with them. I was also journaling with my Inner Child at that time. It was a wonderful combination because I was nurturing my Inner Child and my teachers and guides were nurturing me. I needed a time of quiet cocooning in order to come into greater realization of my own inner power. I gave myself that quiet time each day in my sacred corner.

A sacred corner or sacred room can be of tremendous benefit on our spiritual journey. It is a special place that feels peaceful and protected from distractions. It is helpful to place objects in that sacred space that remind us of our spiritual journey. Many people use a small table to hold the objects. I placed candles and crystals in my sacred corner, as well as my journal. I had a CD player nearby with my favorite meditative music. My sacred corner became the place I read, meditated, journaled, and prayed at least an hour each day.

During those years, Ascended Master Kuthumi, a spiritual light being who has lived on the earth many times, became my spiritual teacher. He led me step by step as I felt more and more connected to my Higher Self and slowly came into a deeper understanding of the healing work I was supposed to do in the world.

My own healing and spiritual growth was my most important work at that time. One day in meditation I saw myself with arms stretched around the world. Master Kuthumi helped me see that the healing I was doing within myself was preparing me to love the world and to teach the world to love. I began to see that what I was really doing in my own healing was learning to love myself. As I loved myself more and more, my clients and students learned to love themselves more. I saw that to teach the world to love meant teaching as many people as I could to love themselves.

Ascended Master Kuthumi was the first spiritual light being who actually sent complete teachings through me in his messages. Receiving messages from spiritual light beings is sometimes called channeling. Although there are various methods of channeling, the one that occurs for me is feeling moved to write what is coming to my mind and heart. But the words are not coming from me. I feel a knowingness deep in my heart that it is Master Kuthumi who is speaking. The words flow out of my fingers, and I almost do not know what the words are until I am finished. The same kind of "flow" happens in most deep creative activity, but in this case the words come from Master Kuthumi.

Ascended Master Kuthumi says: *I come to you today to say that it is important work to make known the part that Ascended Masters and other beings of light have to play in your world today. We are very present to you now. We have chosen to be close to you as you learn how to love and create peace in your world. It is a great day for you as human beings. It is a time of illumination and great progress within the spiritual path of all humans as you learn once again that you are powerful Divine beings who are meant to evolve more quickly now than you ever have before. Great energy is being sent now from the Cosmos to your solar system and to your planet of Terra (planet Earth) to cleanse them as they evolve. That same energy is being sent to you to cleanse yourselves, to heal yourselves, so that you may move into higher spiritual consciousness with us. We are watching and supporting your lives now, and we are sending our own spiritual energy to you in order that you may move forward to peace and unconditional love. Our help is yours for the asking, and we feel your openness at this time to receive our help. Just as the angels are ready now to help you to spiritually awaken more quickly, we who have been humans on the earth and have moved to the higher light realms are ready to guide you in becoming spiritually enlightened. We are actually walking among you again and will make ourselves known in a physical way soon so that you will feel our support in a very tangible way. We love you with a very deep love, and that is why we have chosen the path of staying with you now as you learn who you really are. I send you love and light this day.*

Ascended Master Quan Yin is a spiritual light being who is especially known for her tremendous compassion for all beings living on Mother Earth. She made a personal contact with a client of mine named Melanie who had several serious health problems. Melanie asked for help from the universe after she had tried all that she knew to heal and still did not heal. Soon after that prayer, she was looking at an order blank on the back of a music CD cover. She decided she wanted to order some more music from the same company, so she folded the paper cover and left it on her desk. When she came back to her desk later in the day, she saw that the exact way she had folded the cover revealed a picture of Master Quan Yin on the other side. Melanie knew immediately that Master Quan Yin would help her find answers for her health problems.

Melanie sat down that evening and began communicating with Master Quan Yin in writing. After three days of writing and receiving messages from Master Quan Yin, Melanie followed through on all the messages she received. It was the beginning for Melanie of a completely new approach to healing her body. All of her health problems are healed today. She continues to write to Master Quan Yin and receives ongoing, loving guidance for staying healthy. She feels deep gratitude for Master Quan Yin's loving, compassionate spirit.

> *A sacred corner*
> *or sacred room*
> *can be of tremendous benefit*
> *on our spiritual journey.*

Lord Maitreya is an Ascended Master and the head of the Spiritual Hierarchy for our planet. The Spiritual Hierarchy is the group of all the Ascended Masters from earth. They constantly send energy to all of us on earth for our spiritual evolvement. Much has been written about Lord Maitreya in the last 20 years, as spiritual energy has increased on our planet. He has spoken through channeling, and his message is consistently one of sharing, unity, and peace. He has given many messages of hope amidst the suffering and negativity we find so rampant in the world today. He is physically living on our planet again and is presently living in London.

At this time, Lord Maitreya is showing himself to people who are really ready to hear his message. He is appearing at spiritual gatherings in many countries and is teaching groups of students in London. Although he is not speaking throughout the world yet, he has promised help to anyone who asks for it. When I have needed immediate help with serious problems that seemed to have no solution, I have called on him. Answers within my heart as well as outward solutions have come simultaneously.

When Jann and I traveled to England and Scotland in 2005, we asked him to show himself to us in a physical way if that would be for our highest good. He came to us in the guise of a man who was living on the streets in Glasgow, Scotland. The words of the man in Glasgow went straight to our hearts, and we knew at once it was Maitreya. He showed us a handful of coins and said, "I am a street person, and I am trying to get enough money for a place to stay tonight. I have half of what I need. Can you help me?" His eyes were bright and strong, and we heard Maitreya's message of love and sharing in his words. We gave him some money. He thanked us and we thanked him as we moved apart.

As Maitreya moved down the street, we both had a knowingness that he had indeed come to us that day for our greatest good. It was a confirmation and encouragement to keep teaching love and sharing in order to transform the feelings of separateness and pain in ourselves and in the world.

Spiritual light beings want to support us as we heal and evolve at this critical time in the history of our planet. They are waiting to communicate and teach us lessons we need to learn quickly now as we move into higher-dimensional consciousness with Mother Earth. Our part in that communication is to be open to their messages. The meditation at the end of this chapter is one way for you to begin that process. Once you open your heart to spiritual light beings, you may be happily surprised as you receive the encouragement and blessings they are waiting to bring.

FOR REFLECTION

1. Have you had communication with spiritual light beings? If so, how has that communication helped you?

2. If you have not had communication with spiritual light beings, would you like to? What concerns would you take to them?

MEDITATION
CONNECTING WITH A SPIRITUAL LIGHT BEING

During this meditation you may choose to connect with an angel, an Ascended Master, or another spiritual light being.

1. Choose a quiet place where you will not be interrupted. Sit or lie in a comfortable position and close your eyes. Breathe deeply for a few moments. Notice pain or tension anywhere in your body. Gently breathe into those tense areas, breathing out the tension and pain.

2. Imagine yourself in a beautiful place, a place you have been before or a new place you create. Walk around your place of beauty and experience what you see and smell there. Just be in your beautiful place for the next few moments.

3. Whenever you are ready, ask your spiritual light being to come before you.

4. Say, "I call upon (my companion angel, an Ascended Master) of the light. No etheric beings who are not of the light and part of the universal Divine Plan may be here now. I call only upon a spiritual being of the light." Wait for a feeling of connection in your heart, or visualize your spiritual light being before you.

5. Ask your spiritual light being their name and tell the being you want to connect with them in a special way. Wait for an answer in your heart. It may be through words

or a feeling or a picture. You may or may not learn the name of your spiritual light being the first time you do this meditation. You can do this meditation as often as you wish, and the information and connection will come when it is time.

6. Have a conversation with your spiritual light being, saying anything in your heart you wish to share at this time. Wait for answers and write down anything that comes to you.

7. Finish your conversation by telling your spiritual light being that you want to continue to connect with them and will return to talk again.

CHAPTER FIVE

CONNECTING WITH HIGHER SELF AND LIFE PURPOSE

We come to this planet as human beings to become bridges between spirit and matter. As spiritual beings on a third-dimensional journey, our collective life purpose is to be guardians of Mother Earth and all beings living on her. As we care for and maintain the earth, we and the earth evolve. That is our part in the Divine Plan—the master plan for creation that comes from Divine Source.

Many of us forgot our collective part in the Divine Plan once we arrived on this planet. In order to remember this, our collective life purpose, we have evolved through many lifetimes in which we were able to experience all that would teach us to once again align with our Higher Self. Our Higher Self is the part of us that continually lives in higher consciousness. It is the part of us that never forgets the truth of our part in the Divine Plan.

As we move on the path of spiritual growth and healing, we come to a point when we begin to feel a connection with our Higher Self. Our Higher Self knows our individual life purpose for this lifetime, which is always connected to our collective part in the Divine Plan. Our Higher Self urges us onward to do that work, whether we know it consciously or not.

One way we can become consciously aware of our individual life purpose is through connection with our past lives. I have connected with one of my past lifetimes in which I was part of a group of spiritual light beings who were sent to this earth in order to assist those who were living on the earth at that time. Many earth people of that time had regressed to living in a primitive state. The group of spiritual light beings I belonged to was sent to live among the earth people to help them evolve more quickly.

When we came, we still knew who we were. We felt connected to Divine Source while in physical bodies. We felt connected to the earth and all creation. We did not fear for our survival or fear we were not good enough in any way. We did not fear the loss of things or people or our own power. We knew we would always have everything we needed for our time on earth. We knew we had come for a purpose—to grow through experience and to bring more light into all matter. We were one with our Higher Selves.

Gradually, some of us became more connected to the physical realm than to our Higher Selves. We moved further and further away from our oneness with Divine Source, and we began to feel separate and alone. Fear slowly crept into our lives.

In taking on that fear, we forgot that we were spiritual beings. We moved to a more distant understanding of Divine Source. There were some individuals among us who kept the feeling of connectedness with the Divine, but they had to struggle to maintain that closeness. Wanting to be part of the group pulled at them to move away from oneness with their Higher Selves.

Connecting with that lifetime gave me a deeper understanding of my life purpose in this lifetime, which is to love the world and teach the world to love. I recognized that when I came with that group of beings to the earth so long ago my purpose was similar. I was supposed to help people learn again who they really were so that they could feel love for themselves, for others, and for the earth. They could then become the guardians of the earth they were meant to be.

Connecting with myself in that lifetime gave me strength and understanding to help me follow my life purpose now. It also helped me understand why I had to spend so many years healing myself in this lifetime. I had to heal the feelings of aloneness and separateness and fear I still carried from that lifetime.

Our Higher Self is the part of us that continually lives in higher consciousness.

We go through three different stages in the awareness and development of individual life purpose in the third dimension, and they correspond to how connected we feel to our Higher Self. In the first stage of connection, we are urged by our Higher Self to follow our life purpose without our conscious knowledge or understanding of how that work is connected to the Divine Plan.

Robin was a woman in her early 40s who taught first and second grade throughout her career. She was an excellent teacher and was appreciated both by parents and by school personnel. After nine years of satisfying work, however, the focus of the school district began to change, and Robin found herself disagreeing with the changes. To make matters more difficult, a new principal began at Robin's school whose goals seemed to reflect the goals of the district. Robin felt it was time to consider moving out of the school district and perhaps even teaching a different grade level.

Robin began applying for a new job at nearby school districts, but she had difficulty finding anything that suited her. After some time, she made the decision to stay in her own school district and speak honestly to her new school principal about her philosophy of teaching. Robin was surprised at the outcome. The principal actually shared many of her views about teaching and was in the process of working with the school district to incorporate these views into new policies. The principal asked Robin to assist her with a presentation for the school district.

The presentation they prepared for the school district involved curriculum for the first and second grades. Although Robin did not realize it at the time, she was being guided by her Higher Self to begin the next step of her life purpose, which involved changing the curriculum of the primary grades to include more emotional development.

Since that time, Robin's awareness of her Higher Self and her individual life purpose has expanded, and she has become part of a group of teachers who recommend new curriculum for young children in her school district. She realizes now that the dream of her heart has always been to help children learn in the most holistic way possible. She is now moving into the second stage of awareness of her individual life purpose.

The second big step in awareness and development of our individual life purpose is the process of moving from a more distant understanding of Divine Source to a strong desire for feeling connected to the energy of Divine Source in our everyday lives. At this second stage, we awaken to those characteristics within us that directly come from our Higher Selves. We begin to feel the love and light of our Higher Selves tugging at us, bringing the desire for peace and serenity in the midst of everyday life. Our focus begins to change from outward material goals to the dream of our hearts, our individual life purpose.

Lawrence was a talented and prosperous attorney who had specialized in estate planning for much of his career. His goal was to retire by the age of 50 with enough money to travel and enjoy the rest of his life. However, as he neared retirement, he felt an emptiness within himself and began searching for deeper meaning in his everyday life. He realized that money had not given him the happiness and peace that he thought it would. He shared his feelings with a friend who invited him to a weekly meditation group the friend attended. As Lawrence began meditating he felt a peaceful connection within himself he had never felt before.

During the next year, Lawrence met a number of older people who had lost a spouse and were being financially manipulated by institutions and taken advantage of by individuals in their lives. He began to feel their pain and realized that he had a deep passion for finding ways to legally protect them from harm. He began working with them for much less money than he would ever have accepted before. Money was no longer the primary motivating source in his life.

By the time that Lawrence was 52, he had created a legal advocacy organization that worked to protect seniors from financial opportunists. Today he continues to spread his work as an advocate for seniors in the United States and throughout the world. He has been able to combine his love of travel with his heart's dream to help older people. He is truly enjoying his life. And this all came as a result of his responding to the urgings of his Higher Self. He sees clearly now how his early career and decisions were all steps in his life purpose, very important in themselves and as preparation for this time of service and deep fulfillment.

We go through three different stages
in the awareness and development
of individual life purpose
in the third dimension,
and they correspond to how connected
we feel to our Higher Self.

Terri Ann came to me during the second stage of awareness of her individual life purpose. She told me that she had always been very confident in her interactions with people, whether personal or work related. She had been a waitress for many years and had always felt a special connection with the people she served. She knew now that her life purpose was to connect with ordinary people in her daily life and to feel and send them the energy of love.

As Terri Ann moved into this new awareness of her life purpose, old subconscious pain from the past came up very strongly. This often happens at the second stage of connecting with our life purpose because we cannot move ahead without healing, at a very deep level, any pain that stands in our way. Terri Ann felt that she had completely lost her confidence in interacting with people. She was having serious communication problems in her marriage for the first time and difficulties interacting with co-workers and with some of the new people she had met. She brought her issue of lack of confidence to her sessions with me.

During the next few months, Terri Ann uncovered deep pain from sexual abuse in her childhood. The trauma from the abuse had caused a wound in her self-confidence that she had, until recently, been able to hide from herself. As she became more consciously connected with her life purpose, the old, deep wound surfaced in order to heal.

As she continued the healing process, her self-confidence grew and she connected at a deep, heart level with all the people in her life. In her work as a waitress, she was able to interact with her customers in ways that brought new light into their lives in the short time they were with her. Many customers came to the restaurant more frequently because of her loving energy, and her co-workers were happier because of their interactions with her. Her employer made changes to benefit all who worked for him because of Terri Ann's positive suggestions.

Ascended Master Kuthumi says: *My child, it is important that your readers know the intimate connection between walking the path of the Divine Plan and their contact with their Higher Self in this lifetime. This time in your civilization is crucial to the timely unfolding of the Divine Plan. Your new earth is only created through each individual moving back to oneness. We are all on this path together at this time. The Ascended Masters of your planet are moving with you, assisting you to connect with your Higher Self in your movement back to Source. We are a step ahead of you, leading the way.*

Connecting with your Higher Self in oneness means, in practical terms, living in higher consciousness through seeing and treating as sacred every being in your world. It means understanding that all that exist on your planet are sacred beings in their own right. That includes every blade of grass, every grain in every field, every animal, every insect, and every hurricane or earthquake that moves through your world. It means looking at every being and happening in your world through eyes of light. It means seeing that you and the terrorist are one, even as you and the Christ are one. It means seeing your work in the world as intimately connected to my work and to the work of all Ascended Masters of this world, which is a sacred part of the Divine Plan for this world and for our universe.

If you are meant to bring light to your family through love and communication, you see that as holding a sacred space for your family to evolve. If you are meant to bring light to the homeless or to those in emotional pain, you see that as part of the Divine Plan in which every human being must complete karma and grow into wholeness. You are truly precious to us, your older brothers and sisters, as you make this wondrous journey into light at this unprecedented time in the evolution of our universe. Know that you are guided and held in love each day of your earth lives.

The third stage in following our individual life purpose comes when we have consistently connected with our Higher Self and now are ready to connect consciously at an even higher level. We begin to feel the oneness of all life and to understand that each step of our journey has been connected to our life purpose. We understand how our journey has brought more light into the world, and we see how our individual life purpose is part of the Divine Plan for the earth.

Geraldine was a woman in her late 60s who had been consciously moving on a spiritual path for many years. During her 50s, she worked in therapy to heal many subconscious personality wounds. This work allowed her to realize more easily the dream of her heart. After working as a nurse for 30 years, she moved away from the medical world and began teaching nutrition and herbal healing as her own business. This was during the second stage of awareness of her life purpose.

I met Geraldine at a class I taught in Los Angeles. She came to the class because she felt a huge shift coming in her life and thought it might be a major spiritual transition. During the class, she actually moved into the third stage of connecting with her life purpose as she did the meditations I facilitated during the class. After the second meditation, she shared that she then realized how she had been led by her Higher Self each step of her life to fulfill her higher purpose in this lifetime. She now felt connected to the higher purpose of all human beings on the planet, and she saw clearly how she could fulfill her part in the Divine Plan. She also saw, in that moment, her total connectedness to each created being and their part in the Divine Plan.

The shift that Geraldine made that day was not a shift in mental understanding. It was a shift from thinking about her participation in the oneness of all life to a wordless understanding that comes from pure being. She fell into place with her Higher Self. During the meditations she moved out of concrete thinking and into just being in the present moment— the only place where we can connect with our Higher Self and life purpose. On that day in my class, Geraldine made a leap of connectedness from which there was no turning back. She still experienced times when she moved out of the present moment, but she was able to move back very quickly to her feeling of total connection to her Higher Self and all beings.

> *Connecting with our Higher Self in oneness means, in practical terms, living in higher consciousness through seeing and treating as sacred every being in our world.*

We are connected for all eternity with our Higher Self and with our collective purpose for being on earth as spiritual beings. Feeling that connection comes when we learn to fall into place in that relationship by living in the present moment.

What does it mean to live in the present moment? It cannot be fully described because it is a space in which we move beyond third-dimensional experience. In the present moment we move beyond space, time, and thought. We can practice being open to the present moment, and we can ask to be in the moment. We can sense when we are in the sacred space of the moment, but we cannot truly understand it with our concrete mind.

In the present moment, we are open to just being as well as to the thoughts of our Higher Self. When Geraldine sensed her connection to the higher purpose of all human beings on the planet during meditation, she was in the present moment. It was a sacred space of just being for her that went far beyond her concrete-mind thinking or understanding.

Today we have moved to the point in our evolutionary journey where many more of us on earth are ready to consciously connect with our Higher Self. We are moving through the first two stages of awareness and development of our life purpose at a much greater speed than ever before on this planet. Many more of us want to fully be present, to live in the moment in our daily lives.

One way to be open to the moment is through meditation. The meditative path has been used for eons by human beings seeking to feel connected to their Higher Self. It is still a practical way for many of us today to experience falling into place with our Higher Self. Other very practical and simple ways to help us open to the sacred space of the moment are through the use of mantras, through receiving nature's energy, and through experiencing energy flow.

Mantras are sacred words or phrases that can be easily repeated for an extended period of time. In Eastern religions mantras have been used for centuries to connect with the realms of higher consciousness. We can use known mantras or we can create our own. The mantra replaces the incessant concrete mind chatter that most of us experience throughout our days. Mantra use helps us focus our mind and become open to the sacred space between words.

Some familiar Hindu mantras are "Om" (the primordial sound of the universe), "Om Namah Shivaya" (calling on the Self of all) and "Shanti" (Peace). Familiar Western mantras are "I am," "I am that I am," and "Be still and know that I am God." It is easy to create our own mantras with spiritual words such as "love," "joy," and "presence." Mantras can be sung, chanted, or spoken. They can be used during the quiet time of meditation or to create quiet space at any moment of the day.

Being attentive to nature is another way to open to the sacred space of the moment. Allowing ourselves to experience the energy and beauty of nature helps us feel the connectedness of all beings on our planet. The grass and trees and rivers and streams are members of our earth family who are there for us without questions or conditions. When we listen to their musical sounds or watch their beautiful presence, we can more easily move into the peaceful space between thoughts. They send us their energy even when we do not realize it. If we allow ourselves to feel the energy they send, a space opens up and we can experience just being in the moment.

We can experience energy flow with nature, with people, with animals, and within ourselves. When we look at a sunset, an animal, or another person and sense the beauty deep within that being, we send positive energy to that being. The being receiving energy then sends it back to us. This energy flow can only take place in the moment, and it is in the moment that we experience just being.

The same thing happens during those rare moments when we sense the beauty deep within ourselves. We connect with our Higher Self in those moments. For most of us, these experiences are brief, but this is all that is needed. In those moments we truly feel the connection with our Higher Self and life purpose.

In whatever ways we open to being present in the moment, we open to feeling the connection with our Higher Self and life purpose. In those sacred spaces our concrete mind is silenced and our Higher Self can openly communicate with us. That communication can come in a sensing that goes beyond words, as Geraldine experienced, or in Higher Self thoughts, which are flashes of affirmative words.

Today we have moved to the point
in our evolutionary journey
where many more of us on earth
are ready to consciously
connect with our Higher Self.

Fred came to me for help in completing his grieving after his father's death. He said that he knew his Higher Self could help him finish the grieving. His intention for that first session was to see more clearly how to release his father. Toward the end of our time together, he heard the words "My father and I are one for all eternity. If I connect with myself, I will never lose him."

Fred told me, before he left, that when those words came to him, he felt totally at peace and connected to his Higher Self as well as to his father. I wrote down the words so that he could say them as an affirmation. He spoke the words each day and they became an integral part of completing the grieving process for his father.

These flashes of affirmative words or phrases from our Higher Self can come at any time we allow ourselves to be open to them. They often come when we least expect them, such as when we are taking a shower, shopping for groceries, or driving to work.

Words like "trust yourself," "open your heart," or "just be right now" can give us the support we need to stay out of negative thoughts during daily life circumstances. Today this is happening more easily for many of us, and we are able to move into feeling connected with our Higher Self more quickly than ever before. We can peacefully understand and connect with our individual life purpose.

As we progress through the three stages of development of our individual life purpose, we also come to a deeper understanding of our collective life purpose as spiritual beings on a third-dimensional journey on the earth. That collective purpose is to be guardians of the earth and all beings living on her. That is our part in the Divine Plan. In order to fulfill our collective life purpose, we must first learn to see and treat each being on the earth as a sacred living being.

Our responsibility as guardians includes respect and conservation of earth beings such as water, sun, air, and soil. That means doing our part in keeping pollution from these beings and using them wisely and without harm. It means treating as sacred all beings who grow on the earth, including all trees and grasses and plants and grains. Our part may be to use recycled materials to build in order to save our forests, or it may mean joining with others to find innovative ways to use food surplus to feed people who are hungry. It means not seeing or treating any earth beings as lesser than ourselves. It means feeling our oneness with them, whether they serve our ego needs or not.

Our responsibility as guardians includes seeing and treating as sacred all animal beings. This includes all mammals, all fish, all birds, all insects, and all reptiles. We are meant to be guardians of these beings, and they are meant to be our teachers. Our part may include rescuing a dog or a horse from being killed, becoming part of an activist group to protect the ocean habitats of whales and sea turtles, or finding alternative ways to deal with ants besides killing them. It means not seeing or treating any of these beings as lesser than ourselves. Seeing and treating them as sacred means feeling our oneness with them, no matter if they serve our ego needs or not.

Our collective part in the Divine Plan includes seeing and treating as sacred each person with whom we come in contact. That means our best friends, the people on the freeway who shout obscenities at us, as well as extended family members with whom we have had long-time feuds. It means our spouses and children as well as the clerk at the drug store who took out her problems on us. It means those who are living in poverty as well as those who blame them for living in poverty. It means terrorists and street people and government leaders and ourselves. It means feeling our oneness with them, whether they serve our ego needs or not.

We are each responsible for fulfilling both our role in the collective life purpose of all human beings on the earth and our individual life purpose in this lifetime. Completing our life purpose in this lifetime is necessary in order to move to higher consciousness. It is also our part in bringing light to other beings as they evolve on their path to higher consciousness. Our unique purpose is always about bringing more light into the world. We each have a special combination of spiritual skills, which we are called to use as we create light through connecting with our Higher Self. Our special skills flow from the dream of our heart.

The dream of Robin's heart was to help children find and believe in their dreams. From that dream flowed her skills to provide the changes in curriculum that would bring more light into young children's school lives. Lawrence prepared for many years to use his legal skills to bring more light to older people who needed financial protection. Terri Ann's dream was to feel and send the energy of love to ordinary people in her life. She brought new light into her customers' lives by using her spiritual skills of connecting with people.

What is the dream of your heart? If you see clearly the dream of your heart, then you feel more strongly the connection with your Higher Self who has known that dream for all eternity. If you feel unsure of your dream, your Higher Self is revealing it to you at this very moment. Move out of your thoughts and into the present moment and you will fall into place with your Higher Self.

FOR REFLECTION

1. Walk outside and experience the beauty and energy of nature. Allow yourself to gently move into the peaceful space between thoughts.

2. Watch the sunset or the ocean and see the beauty deep within that being. Send positive energy to the being and allow it to flow back to you.

3. Create your own mantra such as "Love," "Peace," or "Joy." Sing or speak it at different times of an entire day.

MEDITATION
WHAT IS MY LIFE PURPOSE, MY DREAM?

This meditation can be used to more clearly see your individual life purpose through consciously feeling connected to your Higher Self.

1. Find a place to sit where you will not be disturbed for at least 15 minutes. Choose a place that is calming for you, such as a beautiful spot in nature or a room of your home where you feel at peace. Have some paper and a pencil nearby.

2. Sit quietly for a few minutes and breathe deeply.

3. Ask your Higher Self to become more present to you now. When you feel connected to your Higher Self ask, "What is my life purpose, my dream?"

4. Allow the answer to come from your Higher Self in whatever way it comes, in whatever time it takes. It may come in a feeling, a picture, or words. Accept whatever comes.

5. Thank your Higher Self for this gift, and then allow yourself to slowly come back to present time and write down whatever came during the meditation.

CHAPTER SIX

CONNECTING WITH ANIMALS

Ascended Master Kuthumi says: *Our animal brothers and sisters are here to teach us love. Each animal has its special lesson to share with us. Birds teach us to spread our wings and fly. Mother bear teaches us to care for our young, to protect them and teach them to look within. Squirrels teach us to live close to our environment and to trust. They are all parts of us as we are parts of them. Animals are comfortable with being connected. Each species of animal sings the glory of the Creator in its special way, with its special song. Each song is blended into the cosmic song of love that brought us all into form and sustains us as glorious expressions of spirit. Animals understand oneness, and as we move from our individuality into oneness, we can look to them to teach us the way. Animals also look to us to protect them from those humans who would harm them. We have been entrusted with protecting them even as they have been entrusted with teaching us. We are here together to live in mutual trust and assistance. We are here together to love.*

Kris Noel is a beautiful palomino colored colt who was born on December 23, 2005 on our land at Rancho La Puente. He was born during the night, and the next morning one of our granddaughters discovered him standing next to his mother near the barn. Our granddaughter named him Kris Noel because he seemed to be a perfect Christmas gift for all of us. A few days after Kris Noel was born, we held a healing gathering at the ranch. During that gathering Jann received the message from her Higher Self that Kris Noel had come into this world to bring Christ consciousness to the land at Rancho La Puente and to the part of New Mexico where the ranch is located.

We knew Kris Noel was special because he immediately began demonstrating behaviors that were very unusual for foals. After nursing from his mother, Centauri, he nursed from another mare, Raven, who is the leader of our mares. This sharing seemed to be totally acceptable to his mother and the other mares. He also started eating his own little pile of alfalfa at less than a week of age. The usual behavior among a group of horses is for the dominant horses to push the younger ones away and eat first. The other horses did not disturb Kris Noel or try to eat from his pile. We humans at the ranch continue to be inspired by his lessons of personal power and sharing.

In a two-week period between August 29 and the middle of September, three other foals had been born on the land: one colt and two fillies, each with a unique story to tell. One of these was the foal of our mare, Tsalagi. One night when Tsalagi was close to giving birth, she seemed reluctant to stay in her stall, so a young man who was working at the ranch drove out into the field where she seemed to be leading him. He kept the car lights on and lay down near her to keep vigil. He fell asleep for a while until something startled him awake. He saw that Tsalagi was in deep labor and was having trouble. She looked him straight in the eye and he heard her plea for help. He delivered the foal having had no previous experience with horses. Ocoee, her foal, is now a healthy and beautiful colt.

There are 13 horses in all at the ranch, most of whom we have rescued or have been brought to the ranch for healing. Some stay for short periods of time if there is a right and loving home for them on other land. Some stay for the rest of their lives if that is where they are supposed to be. Each horse comes with messages and teaching for us and for those humans who come to our land for healing and inner growth.

Animals understand oneness,
and as we move from
our individuality into oneness,
we can look to them
to teach us the way.

Our spiritual journey is about connectedness. It is about learning and growing in the knowledge that we are intimately connected to all other beings, whether they are humans, spiritual light beings, animals, the earth and all vegetation that grows on the earth, or planets and solar systems in our galaxy and other galaxies.

We each have our individual path on that spiritual journey, and our teachers on that unique path are beings who touch us deeply along the way and have messages for us that can help us grow. Our closest companions, whether they are humans or animals or spiritual light beings, are usually the most significant teachers we have. They are with us on a daily basis, bringing their energy to us, revealing themselves to us, teaching us, and learning from us as we bring the same to them.

Animals may meet us on our path when we are ready to hear certain messages from them. One night some years ago, my ex-husband Victor and I were driving at night on a road overlooking the ocean. We had been in conversation about a change we were making in our work in the world. All of a sudden, seemingly from nowhere, an owl landed on our windshield and looked us in the eyes for some moments. We jumped in surprise and concern that she might be hurt. After looking at us, she turned and flew away. It was then that we knew she was not hurt and that, instead, she was sending us the message: "Make your decisions in wisdom and truth." We never saw her again. She had come to us at a moment of need as teachers do.

Animals are our companions and our teachers. They teach us to connect with ourselves as spiritual beings. They also teach us how to reconnect with our role as guardians of the earth. Each animal teaches us aspects of our spiritual selves that we must integrate as we go about remembering who we really are. Some teach us to live in the moment and to trust life. Some teach us to live in peace and love. They can teach us how to share power and how to face our fears. If we open our hearts to them, they will teach us how to heal. I have included a list of animals and some of the gifts they bring to humans in Appendix A.

Whales and dolphins are fully conscious aquatic beings whose ancestors were land mammals who had evolved to a high sentient level and had created an agrarian civilization. The ancestors were training to become the first physical land guardians of the earth. When their civilization was threatened to extinction by warring forces from other planets, they decided that many of them would have to leave the planet and the rest would learn to live in the oceans. In this way, they could become guardians of the earth's water realms and still watch over the land until other land guardians were appointed. These beings evolved into the whales and dolphins of today. They have remained guardians of the earth and will do so until we humans are ready to take over that assignment as fully conscious beings.

The great whales create the electrical energy patterns of song that preserve life year after year in the waters around our earth. They sing a note of very high frequency that balances and strengthens our oceans. The dolphins channel that energy to individual species to maintain their existence. The great whales and dolphins are with us also to teach us each to sing our own song, the song of our uniqueness as we evolve into fully conscious beings of joy and planetary responsibility.

For eons, whales and dolphins have sent humans important messages to help us awaken to our love connection with all other beings. At this special time in our human evolution, they are even more urgently drawing us to hear their messages. My partner Jann had been drawn to visit Stonehenge for many years, and she was finally able to visit there in July of 2005. While there, she received a channeling from the whales' higher collective consciousness: "This monument was not made by humans. It was created by whales over 10,000 years ago. We thought it into being. To us it is a love ring. It is a configuration that brings a concentration of love to it. We built it to connect to the human beings on land, to help them raise their consciousness level and become more aware of their connection to the earth and the cosmos. This love ring was a gift from those of higher consciousness to those who would be able to evolve into greater consciousness."

Each animal teaches us aspects of our
spiritual selves that we must integrate
as we go about remembering
who we really are.

Eileen is a friend of mine who shared with me her experience of receiving loving connection and support from dolphins. She was invited to go to Hawaii by a group that regularly swims with dolphins. She had felt a kinship with dolphins all her life, so when the invitation came from the group, she was excited and decided to go immediately. However, she knew she would have to face her fear of the water.

The group arrived on the Big Island of Hawaii and spent the night camping on the beach. The next morning, as Eileen put her face in the water, waves of panic came over her. She felt as if she were drowning. Her companions stayed with her in loving support. They cradled her and coached her as she floated along. Finally, she heard the dolphins all around her and found herself becoming calm and settling in to the rhythm of the sea.

The next day, when Eileen went into the water, she could see the dolphins at a distance. She sensed waves of strong, loving energy coming from them as they moved closer to her. She relaxed in the water and found herself swimming and playing with the dolphins.

This whole experience with the dolphins led to great healing for Eileen. When she returned from the trip, she felt a stronger confidence and sense of self, and she also felt a much greater ability to feel compassion for herself and others. She could let herself relax and play more than ever before.

Animals can teach us how to share power and how to face our fears.

Elephants became land guardians of the earth later in earth's history after the ancestors of the whales and dolphins had moved to the oceans. They have lived for eons in large communal groups in order to sing their deep song. Their song creates electrical energy patterns that balance and strengthen the earth in a continual symphony of sound. Their deep song provides the framework in which each land animal species can sing its own song and maintain its existence. The elephants do for the land what the whales and dolphins do for the waters around our land. Elephants are also our earth historians. They carry the story of the earth from the time of its creation up to the present day. They carry that story for all of us so that the story itself becomes part of the deep web of consciousness that connects each of us humans to one another and to all other species on our land.

Sadly, since elephants have been torn from their homes in the wild and have been abused by humans, they have struggled to continue to sing their deep song. They sing their song in smaller groups now, and many times they are forced to live alone in captivity. While in captivity, they send messages to any sensitive earth humans who can hear them. Even though they cannot sing their song in captivity, they are taking this opportunity to warn us that we are harming the earth in devastating ways. If we continue on this path, Mother Earth could be permanently damaged and life on her surface would end. If the great whales, the dolphins, and the elephants are not allowed to sing their songs, the lives of thousands of species in our oceans and on our land will be seriously endangered.

Horses teach us about safe movement and freedom. The ancestor of the modern horse was eohippus, a small horse-like mammal that lived in North America. Over eons of time, that ancestor moved across the Bering Strait, grew larger through evolution, and became the modern horse that was brought back to this land by the Spanish in the 1500s.

Horses live naturally in a nomadic society. They can teach us about the fluidity and freedom to be ourselves instead of being pulled down into a sedentary and static existence. They teach us about the power of becoming lighter.

Horses are powerful healers who seek balance and congruency. They show us how to heal the unexpressed emotions we hold within. We have been taught in our civilization to seek approval and safety through the suppression of feelings. Horses help us find spiritual safety and freedom through the expression of feelings. They do not accept masks. They are experts at feeling and mirroring any hidden emotions that human beings around them are carrying. They have learned to perceive emotions at a distance, so they know our feelings at a gut level, even if we try to cover them up.

If you walk up to a horse with a smile on your face while suppressing strong anger, fear, or sadness, the horse will begin to feel unsafe and anxious. If you acknowledge those same feelings, the horse will begin to feel calmer. You will feel the calmness and balance from speaking your truth, and you will feel the calmness and restored balance coming from the horse's body as well.

Because of the tremendous healing that can come from connecting with horses, a number of equine therapy centers are opening all over the United States. People who have suffered sexual, physical, and emotional abuse are healing by connecting with these spiritually sensitive beings. Many times horses who have been abused become healers who finally touch the souls of human beings who feel broken in spirit.

Humans who visit Rancho La Puente experience the healing energy of our horses even if they never ride one. They can interact with the horses and learn to care for them and feed them. As people spend time around our horses, they experience an exchange of positive energy with the horses and find themselves just being in the present moment. Even watching the horses grazing from the windows of our homes brings feelings of peace and contentment to all of us living at the ranch.

What about our beloved dogs and cats? Many of us do not have everyday contact with whales and dolphins, elephants or horses, but our dogs and cats are with us constantly as our teachers, companions, and healers. Dogs are especially good mirrors for those human beings whom they love and who are their companions. They bond deeply with us and sometimes act out our own pain and fear. They seem to carry it for us so that we can learn the lessons that are most difficult for us to learn. They teach us unconditional love, loyalty, and service.

Our beloved dog, Oso, has consistently been there for us at the ranch, helping us see those truths within ourselves that we have had most difficulty seeing. He has taught us to love ourselves more deeply through his constant love and loyalty toward us. He is always of service, whether that means bringing a litter of homeless kittens to Victor to raise, guiding visitors on tours of the ranch, or spending time with people who need to heal.

Gina came to the ranch for a weekend retreat. She had very little experience being away from cities and no experience with being close to animals. In fact, she had an old fear of animals, especially dogs. Oso spent a lot of time with her, sitting with her, looking at her with his beautiful loving eyes. At first, Gina reacted by trying to move away from him, but Oso kept following her until she allowed herself to be in his presence. Then he took long walks with her, making a path for her when the other animals began to gather around her. She was not ready for interaction with several animals at once, and Oso made sure that she never had more than she could handle. By the time she left Rancho La Puente, she had had a very good experience riding a horse, and she decided she really did like dogs. She made plans to return to the ranch in order to spend more time with the animals.

Our domestic cats, as well as lions and tigers on our earth, are related to the fully conscious lion-like beings who inhabit a planet in the Sirius star system. Our cats inherit from them a highly sensitive and intelligent nature that understands the wisdom of a simple life. They teach us the healthy life balance of companionship, independence, and play.

Marita was the only child of parents who had serious marital problems. She felt very lonely because of the discord, and after traumatic incidents with her verbally abusive father, she felt despondent and afraid. At nine years of age, she had friends at school but did not feel comfortable bringing them to her home. When she came home from school each day, she felt tremendous loneliness.

Marita's mother heard of an opportunity to adopt a kitten and decided to do so. Marita was very excited. She could hardly wait for the tiny being to become her companion. At the last minute, however, the woman who was going to offer the kitten decided to give it to another family. Marita was very upset. Her mother promised that she would begin looking for another kitten. The next day a co-worker told Marita's mother about a kitten she had found and had been feeding for about a week near the office parking lot. She suggested that Marita's mother take the kitten home. Marita named the kitten Boots because she had little white boots on her beautiful black-and-white body.

Marita and Boots were inseparable whenever Marita was home. Each day when she got home from school, Marita and Boots would play "Kitty Chase" and other games they created together. She had the companionship she so greatly needed at home, and slowly she began inviting her friends over to play. Much of the play was done in the company of Boots.

Many of us do not have
everyday contact with whales
and dolphins, elephants or horses,
but our dogs and cats are with us constantly
as our teachers, companions,
and healers.

Animals are telepathic and send messages that are direct and to the point. For most humans, it takes practice to open up telepathic channels wide enough to speak and listen fully at that level. However, since that ability is within all of us and needs to be developed in order to evolve spiritually, communicating with animals is a rewarding and easy way to practice. Eventually our communication with other humans will also be mostly telepathic with a minimum of words needed.

Many times animals communicate telepathically with humans without human request. If you are open to receive the message, you will hear within what you need to hear at that time. Such was the case with the owl I mentioned earlier. Other times human beings choose consciously to receive spiritual learning from animals. In order to connect with an animal at a spiritual level, allow yourself to be drawn to a certain animal intuitively. It may be an animal who passed you in your life one day. It may be an animal companion with whom you have been bonded for years. It may be an animal to whom you feel drawn for no apparent reason. You can practice connecting spiritually with the animal you choose by using the meditation at the end of this chapter.

Our collective life purpose as human beings is to be guardians of Mother Earth and all beings who live on her. This includes all animals. We are meant to be their guardians and they are meant to be our teachers. Animals understand oneness and they will teach us the way to oneness if we learn to live with them in mutual trust and love. As we provide the space for animals to sing their songs, we can learn to sing our own special songs, joining our voices with theirs in the cosmic song of love.

FOR REFLECTION

1. Is there an animal in your life with whom you have a bonded relationship at this time? What are you learning from that animal?

2. Review Appendix A. Have you received messages from any of these animals? What lessons have you learned from them?

3. Spend a short period of time with an animal (15 – 20 minutes). Allow yourself to just be in the present moment. What impressions and feelings do you have?

MEDITATION
CONNECTING WITH AN ANIMAL AT THE SPIRITUAL LEVEL

Before you begin this meditation, choose an animal with whom you wish to connect with at the spiritual level. It can be an animal companion who lives with you, or it can be any animal with whom you wish to connect, whether you have ever seen that animal or not.

1.   Get into a comfortable position and close your eyes… feel any pain or tension anywhere in your body…breathe into those tense parts, and breathe out the tension… just notice your breath and let go of the outer world. You have nothing you have to do now and nowhere you have to go.

2.   Imagine yourself standing on a beautiful spot on the earth…now imagine a huge rock deep in the center of the earth…imagine its vivid colors…rich, earthy colors such as reds, oranges, and yellows…imagine energy vibrating from the rock, and see it as waves of light or feel it as a gentle pulse, the heartbeat of the earth.

3.   Now focus on your breathing, and as you inhale, imagine you are breathing in the waves of energy that are spiraling upward from the heart of the earth…draw the earth energy up through your feet and legs into your pelvis… breathe deeply, allowing the rich colors of the earth energy to fill your spine.

4. Let the energy then fill your entire body as you continue to breathe...when you feel or sense the energy completely filling your body, let it move outside your body, surrounding you with the vibrant colors of the earth.

5. Imagine the energy from the heavens as a warm golden sun above your head...as you breathe in, imagine you are breathing in this golden spiritual light...see or sense your whole body filling with the light...let the light move outside your body and surround you with its radiant glow...let the light draw you upward to a world of radiant, shimmering, sparkling light—the spiritual plane of existence... It is here that you will connect with the animal you have chosen.

6. Whenever you are ready, allow yourself to see, feel, or sense your chosen animal moving toward you...greet your animal and send the energy of love to the animal...spend a few moments just being together. Allow yourself to know why you chose to be with this animal, either for this meditation or for a longer period of time in your life.

7. Talk to your chosen animal, asking why they chose you, and tell the animal why you chose them at this time in your life. Talking and answering at the spiritual level can be in pictures, feelings, or even words...complete the conversation, asking or telling the animal anything else you want to say at this time.

8. Thank your animal for sharing with you today, and begin slowly coming back to present time, knowing that you can connect with the animal again if you wish...breathe deeply and feel your body coming back to present time... write anything you wish to remember, such as why your animal and you chose each other at this time.

CHAPTER SEVEN

CONNECTING WITH UNIVERSAL LIFE FORCE ENERGY

Universal Life Force Energy is the energy that gives us life. It is the energy that flows through all life forms here on earth and everywhere in our solar system, our galaxy, and our universe. It is the energy that the great whales hold in their care as guardians in our oceans, and it is the energy that dolphins direct to all life forms living in the oceans. It is the energy that flows through each plant and flower and tree on our magnificent planet. It moves through the rocks and the rivers, the rain and the rainbows, the rays of the sun and the light of the moon. Universal Life Force Energy is the song that the elephants sing as guardians of the earth, and it is the music we humans sing on earth that connects us to the higher dimensions.

Universal Life Force Energy has been used in healing since the beginning of time. It has been used by Native American healers and indigenous healers in all parts of the world for hands-on energy healing as well as for the long-distance healing of body, mind, emotions, and spirit.

One of the men who searched for a way to use Universal Life Force Energy for healing was Dr. Mikao Usui. Dr. Usui was born in a small village near Kyoto, Japan in 1865, a time when Japan was going through a period of rapid change. Until 1850, Japan had been isolated from the outside world. As Japan opened its borders and began the process of industrialization, a climate developed in which people wanted to revive and maintain ancient traditions while integrating the new. This climate of openness paved the way for the interest and practice of hands-on energy healing to grow and become accepted in many areas of Japan.

There are several different versions of Dr. Usui's life story because much of what we have learned has come through oral tradition. The following story is one of those versions. Dr. Usui grew up in a Tendai Buddhist family and began his schooling at a Tendai Buddhist monastery when he was four years old. Tendai Buddhism is an ancient form of Buddhism that came to Japan from China in the eighth century. As part of his training in the monastery, Usui learned Kiko—a health and healing discipline based on the development and use of Universal Life Force Energy. Young Usui noticed that Kiko required the build-up and then the depletion of one's own life energy when doing healing work. This sparked a curiosity in Usui about the possibility of doing healing work without depleting one's own energy. To research this possibility, Usui studied medicine, psychology, and the theology of world religions. He traveled to China, Europe, and the United States for many of his study experiences.

Usui married and had two children and followed a number of professions: public servant, reporter, politician's secretary, industrialist, and missionary. For a period of time, he was a Tendai Buddhist monk but remained at home with his family. However, later in his life, after studying with Christian missionaries, he became a Christian, a minister, and the dean of a small Christian university in Kyoto.

During the time that Usui was a dean at the university, several of his students came to him and asked him about the physical healings of Jesus. The students reminded Usui that Jesus had said, "You will do as I have done, and even greater things" (see John 14:12). The students wanted to know why there were not more healers doing the same kind of healing, and they asked Usui to teach them how to do it. Feeling bound by his honor to answer their questions, Usui was faced with his limitation and so resigned his position at the university. He left the university determined to find the answer to the mystery of healing.

As part of his quest to find the answers, Usui studied in the Theological Seminary at the University of Chicago. However, he did not find the answers he was looking for, so he returned to Japan and traveled to several Buddhist monasteries searching for records of Buddha's healings of the body. The abbots of the monasteries all told him that the focus was now on spiritual healing rather than the healing of the body.

The abbot of the monastery where he had studied as a child was the most encouraging. He suggested that Usui keep studying to find the answer. As a result, Usui studied Chinese and Sanskrit so that he could read the ancient sacred manuscripts. He then traveled to the Himalayas and found records of healings done by St. Isa in India, who some scholars believe was Jesus.

After his travels and studies of the ancient texts, Usui felt that he intellectually understood the healings of Jesus. He then returned to Japan and immediately went to talk to the abbot who had encouraged him and asked how he might receive the empowerment to heal as Jesus did. The abbot and Usui prayed and meditated together. From this time of reflection, Usui decided that he would begin a 21-day fast and retreat on Mt. Kurama.

On the last day of his fast before dawn, Usui prayed for an answer to come. He looked to the sky and saw a flicker of light, which was growing and moving toward him. It proceeded to strike him in the center of his forehead, and he saw beautiful bubbles of light that turned into sacred Sanskrit symbols. He then felt tremendous energy coming into the crown of his head. He knew at once that the answer to his prayer had come.

Usui then received the message that both Buddha and Jesus had allowed a tremendous inflowing of Universal Life Force Energy into their bodies. The energy moved in through the crown of their heads, down into their hearts, and out through their hands to heal people. Their energy was never depleted because as they healed, they continually received more energy. It was a never-ending flow. The message also came to Usui that if he visualized the ancient Sanskrit symbols while healing, the strength of the energy would increase. Usui felt ready to begin using Universal Life Force Energy to do healing work and called this healing energy Reiki, which means "Spiritually Guided Universal Life Force Energy."

Usui did Reiki healing work for the next seven years among the poor in Kyoto. He hoped to help street people integrate back into society. Some of them did, but many of them eventually came back to the streets to live. Usui then realized that healing requires responsibility on the part of those receiving it. The responsibility involves two things. It requires a person to ask for the healing, and it requires an equal exchange of energy. This equal exchange of energy means that the person receiving Reiki needs to give something back for the healer's time. This can take place in the form of money or another agreed upon barter. Usui took this understanding into all of his future work.

Usui began to teach Reiki healing throughout Japan and trained other teachers to continue this healing work. He also opened a Reiki clinic in Tokyo. Shortly before his death in 1926 he asked one of his most devoted teachers, Chujiro Hayashi, to carry on his work. It was Dr. Hayashi who took Reiki healing to Hawaii at the request of one of his own Reiki students, Hawayo Takata.

Mrs. Takata was born in 1900 on the island of Kauai, Hawaii. She traveled to Japan for medical treatment for gallstones, appendicitis, and a tumor. While in Japan, she heard about Dr. Hayashi's Reiki clinic and decided to go there before her scheduled surgery. All of her health problems were healed through Reiki, and she decided to learn this amazing healing practice for herself. After studying under Dr. Hayashi, Mrs. Takata began teaching in Hawaii. It is from her that Reiki came to the United States.

> *Universal Life Force Energy*
> *has been used in healing*
> *since the beginning of time.*

Reiki heals by balancing the energy centers, or chakras, of the body. *Chakra* is a Sanskrit word that means "spinning wheel." Chakras function to distribute and maintain energy throughout the physical body and the other three bodies of our four-body system.

Outside the physical body is the human aura or energy field of light. In this aura, there are three areas, sometimes called the emotional body, the mental body, and the spiritual body. Since the chakras distribute and maintain energy for these bodies as well as the physical body, the energy generated by these centers nourishes our physical, emotional, mental, and spiritual aspects as human beings. Some of the major chakras are:

1. First Chakra—located at the base of the tailbone—

contains the energy of connection to the earth, to security, and our relationship to the physical body

2. Second Chakra—located halfway between the navel and the groin areas—contains the energy of sexuality, creativity, and nurturing. It holds the energy of our first relationships in childhood

3. Solar Plexus Chakra—located just under the rib cage—holds the energy of power and the expression of emotions

4. Heart Chakra—located in the center of the chest—holds the energy of love for self and others

5. Throat Chakra—located in the center of the throat—holds the energy of self-expression and communication

6. Third-eye Chakra—located between the eyebrows on the forehead—contains the energy of intuition and higher wisdom

7. Crown Chakra—located on the top of the head—brings in spiritual energy from the higher dimensions and connects us to Divine Source

When I began Reiki healing with clients, I found that they were able to receive and utilize the greater influx of Universal Life Force Energy to heal their physical bodies. I also noticed that their emotional, mental, and spiritual issues healed more quickly than ever before. I have yet to find any form of healing that works as quickly, powerfully, and completely as Reiki.

A typical Reiki healing session with me lasts about an hour. I begin by talking to the person receiving Reiki about what they wish to heal during that time. If they have not had Reiki healing before, I explain to them how Reiki energy comes into my body from the universe, moves through me, and out my hands for healing. I also explain how I read the body's energy field with a pendulum made from semi-precious stones. The person then lies on a massage table in a peaceful environment.

When the person is comfortable, I extend the pendulum above each chakra, reading the electro-magnetic energy of the body to determine if their chakras are open and balanced. The chakras that are closed indicate constricted or stuck energy that needs to be cleared. This gives the person receiving Reiki a sense of how their physical body is responding to the issues they wish to heal. After sharing the results with the person, I begin sending Reiki healing energy from the universe into their body. I do this either with my hands on or above the different chakras of the body.

Toward the end of the session, I again check all the chakras with the pendulum to determine if any chakra needs additional energy. When all chakras are open and balanced, I have the person remain on the table until they feel ready to sit up. I then talk to them about their experience and, when they are comfortable, I end the session.

Reiki heals by balancing the energy centers, or chakras, of the body.

June came to me because she felt disconnected from God and from the people in her life. She worked alone as a computer programmer, and had lived alone in the five years since her divorce. Both of her grown children lived in Europe, and she had little contact with them. She had no contact with her ex-husband after what was a very painful divorce. She felt she no longer had anything in common with her friends and rarely saw them. June was very lonely and wanted to change but did not know how.

At one of our initial sessions, I told her about the power of Reiki to heal emotional issues through balancing the energy in all of our chakras. She said that she welcomed the chance to heal energetically because she spent most of her daily life in left-brain activities. The left side of the brain in the human body is used for linear thinking, analyzing, and planning. The right side of the brain is used for intuition and creativity. Reiki healing helps to balance both sides of the brain so that the person can use their whole brain to make changes in their life.

I worked with June privately for a year. I gave her weekly Reiki healing sessions during which several deep emotional issues came up for her. The loneliness issue was one that went back to her childhood. Her mother died when she was very young and her father sent her to live with relatives that took good care of her physically but did not connect with her emotionally. Through Reiki energy June was able to get in touch with the devastating pain of abandonment and loneliness that she felt as a child.

I combined Inner Child work with Reiki, and June was able to acknowledge her inner pain, express it, and allow it to move through her and out of her body. She had carried the pain in the back of her heart chakra and in her second chakra. As the stuck energy moved out of those two areas, June was able to get in touch with several past lives in which she found loneliness scenarios similar to the ones she had experienced in this lifetime. By healing the pattern of loneliness that she lived in those lifetimes, she was able to heal the same pattern in this lifetime.

June has now studied all levels of Reiki and is using Reiki with herself, clients, family, and friends. She is now in close contact with her adult children, and she has a new circle of friends who share her love for healing and connectedness.

Reiki healing helps to balance both sides of the brain so that the person can use their whole brain to make changes in their life.

Vivian came to me for Reiki treatments because she had severe migraine headaches that were becoming worse and keeping her from functioning in daily life. A friend of hers had healed her migraines through a series of Reiki treatments from others and by doing Reiki on herself every day. Vivian hoped that Reiki would help her as much as it had her friend. As I worked with her, it became clear to Vivian and to me that the migraines were connected to tremendous stress in her life that came from old emotional pain. The reason that the headaches were increasing in intensity at that time was that circumstances in her life were triggering the old pain.

Vivian had recently begun working for a company that she really liked. She felt the position was one that fit her personality and her goals. The only problem was that, in her particular department, she found a daily reenactment of the drama she experienced in her family when growing up. Her immediate supervisor was very much like her emotionally abusive and controlling mother. Her supervisor's boss was very similar in looks and manner to her raging, alcoholic father. One of her co-workers had the same angry, abusive manner as her older sister.

Vivian had not healed the childhood pain connected with the dysfunction in her family, so she easily assumed the role of peacemaker—a role that she had taken on as a child. It did not work in her new environment just as it had not worked for her as a child. Because of this, she began to take the stress of other people's issues into her own body, and her migraines came on with fierce strength.

Vivian focused on both physical and emotional healing during her Reiki sessions, and we discovered that she had a great deal of energy stuck in her third-eye chakra and her second chakra. I did many Belief/Fear Release exercises with her during the Reiki sessions. Through this she was able to release the fears that caused her to repeat the self-defeating patterns she had learned in childhood for survival purposes. As she released those fears, the physical pain and stuck energy in her third eye lessened. The constricted energy in her second chakra released, and she began to practice new ways of interacting at work. Her need for the old peacemaker role was gone.

I also taught Vivian how to do self-healing with a shortcut method I teach my students and clients. It consists of four hand positions that bring Reiki energy into the entire body, and it can be done in a very short time. While placing the hands on each area of the body, all that is needed is to think "Reiki." People take two minutes, five minutes, or any amount of time they wish on each area. Vivian found that the shortcut gave her great physical and emotional relief and peace. She did Reiki on herself everyday and also came to my monthly Reiki healing circles in which we all give and receive Reiki. In addition to this, she kept coming for weekly Reiki sessions with me.

Vivian's migraines today are completely gone, and she is able to focus on the work that supports her goals and unique talents. The people she works with still have their issues with control and anger, but Vivian has learned to speak her truth to them and not allow their negativity into her body and emotions. She no longer accepts abuse of any kind in her life.

Reiki healing is the fastest and most complete way I know to move through the deep physical and emotional cleansing we humans are all experiencing today as we move into higher consciousness with Mother Earth. Through Reiki we can allow into our hearts the tremendous amount of light we need in order to remember our song of oneness with Divine Source.

FOR REFLECTION

1. Are you interested in experiencing Reiki healing energy? If so, you can use the meditation at the end of this chapter to allow that energy to flow into your body through your own hands.

2. Are you interested in other experiences with Reiki healing energy? If you are, you can look for Reiki Practitioners on the Internet, in the Yellow Pages of your phone book, and in alternative-health resource directories.

MEDITATION
REIKI SHORTCUT EXERCISE

For the following exercise, many people enjoy listening to soft, meditative music. If you wish, begin playing that type of music in the background. If you prefer, allow yourself to be in silence. Sit or lie in a comfortable place where you will not be disturbed for about fifteen minutes. In all of the following positions, you will place your hands on your body with your fingers together. Use your intuition to guide you in the length of time you remain in each position.

1. Begin by placing one hand on your crown chakra (top of head) and the other on your throat chakra (throat). Think "Reiki" and the Reiki energy will begin to flow into you from the universe. Keep your hands there as long as you wish.

2. Next place one hand on your third eye (forehead) and the other on the back of your throat chakra (back of neck). It is not necessary to think "Reiki" again during this exercise. It begins flowing the first time you think it and will continue as long as you are doing the exercise. Keep your hands there as long as you wish.

3. Then place one hand on your heart chakra (center of chest) and one hand on your solar plexus chakra (under the rib cage in the center of the body). Keep your hands there as long as you wish.

4. Lastly, place both your hands on your first and second chakras (hands beginning at the level of the hips facing inward and downward toward the pubic bone). Keep your hands there as long as you wish.

5. When you have completed all the positions, continue to sit or lie quietly for several minutes. When you feel ready, slowly get up and peacefully go on with your day.

CHAPTER EIGHT

CONNECTING WITH EARTH ENERGY AND ABUNDANCE

The earth is a living, breathing sacred being with chakras, or energy centers, just as are all beings who live on the earth. Many ancient peoples named the living spirit of the earth and considered her a goddess. This goddess was known as Tellus for the Romans and Gaia for the Greeks. She was the inner, higher-dimensional spirit of planet earth.

Although most of us still experience earth as only third dimensional, our sacred planet is actually multi-dimensional, as we are, with the sacred energy of many dimensions surging through it. Twelve dimensions actually exist on planet earth, and we need and utilize all the dimensions to carry out our life on earth.

Dimensions are simply levels of consciousness that organize existence through the use of energy. For example, first dimension on the earth is the dimension of pure minerals. Each mineral has its unique vibration and is a conduit for energy coming from higher dimensions. Second dimension is the realm of bacteria and other simple life forms.

Third dimension has been the dimension of all conscious life on earth for millennia. It has given structure to human, animal, and plant interaction on Mother Earth. Third dimension has a slowed-down speed of vibration that allows everything around us to seem solid. Nothing, including the human body, is truly solid but rather is an energy-flowing form created from light. We have needed a world that appears solid in order to experience the manifestation of creation at a material level. In the third dimension, we have learned the power of our personalities to make things happen. We have established belief systems to use the energy of our concrete minds to find ways to take action in the world. Those belief systems became customs, technology, institutions, and religions. We have used them to benefit ourselves and others, and we have used them to destroy ourselves and others.

One big difficulty with the third dimension is that, because energy is moving at such a slowed-down rate, it is easier for energy to get stuck, both in ourselves and in the outside world. It takes great effort to keep our thoughts and feelings aligned so that we can take appropriate actions to manifest our goals. We can get stuck in negative feelings and thoughts and choose actions that harm ourselves and other beings. And earth takes on the energy of the beings living on her. Since human beings have expressed a tremendous amount of negative energy over the millennia, Mother Earth has many places on her surface and within her body that need healing at this time.

Our sacred planet is multi-dimensional, as we are, with the sacred energy of many dimensions surging through it.

The energy of Mother Earth, also called telluric energy since Roman times, connects with Universal Life Force Energy through systems very much like the human nervous and chakra systems. Our universe supports Mother Earth, as it supports all beings living on her, by continually sending multi-dimensional sacred life force energy into her etheric body or aura. That sacred energy can then enter her physical body through chakras and other centers called portals, or interdimensional windows. This provides sustenance and healing for Mother Earth and for all beings living on her.

Telluric energy moves through our planet in electromagnetic currents called ley lines. This powerful sacred energy is the nervous system of our earth. Ley lines are usually located near other natural telluric energy conduits, such as lakes and rivers, mountains and volcanoes, and in minerals such as quartz. This energy can be felt by humans, animals, and plants as nourishing, calming, and healing.

At certain locations along the ley lines, there are vortexes of intense circular-motion energy that continually feed Mother Earth from her higher dimensions and from the universe. Mother Earth and all of us, her children, need this special replenishing at this significant time before 2012.

At that time the earth will take the huge leap of moving into the Age of Light. We have the opportunity to move with Mother Earth as she takes this leap. Third dimension will then no longer be part of life on earth. Many of us are now learning to more consciously access Mother Earth's fourth-and fifth-dimensional energies. As we learn, we move in and out of that flow each day.

Fourth dimension is the dimension of flow. In this dimension, energy is speeded up enough for life to move easily. In fourth dimension, we easily fall into place with our Higher Self and higher purpose in life. Living in the moment is no longer a struggle. The use of power is directed by the flow of our Higher Self instead of our concrete mind. Our Higher Self guides us to use our personality in the most appropriate ways to act in our world. We are able to recognize the Divine Plan in creation and see how to create only those groups and communities that bring the law of love into the world.

In fifth dimension, the electrical flow of energy is greatly increased. It is the dimension of all creating on earth. When we follow our higher purpose, we are actually co-creating with Divine Source through the guidance of our Higher Self. We then manifest that creation in fourth and third dimensions. For example, this book was created in fifth dimension. It was the result of my Higher Self's vision. The creation then moved into the flow in fourth dimension as my Higher Self guided me to put actual words on paper. It will finally be fully manifested in third dimension when it is printed.

I asked Lord Maitreya how the higher dimensions in our solar system and on Mother Earth work together for creation. He answered: *It is very important for humans to understand how the higher dimensions in your world come together for creation. Dimensions are not one above another—in stepladder fashion—as many imagine them to be. They swirl around in an elliptical manner, very close to one another, connected and interdependent with each other. If you could view ninth dimensional energy at this moment, you would see swirling strands of crystalline white light that is the beginning of actual creation in your world. That crystalline light is now moving at an accelerated pace into your world for the energy of Ascension. It has always been there, though, for creation of all that is needed for your earth and for all life forms on it to exist. That Divine crystalline light becomes beautiful flowing patterns of color in eighth dimension, opening endless possibilities for co-creation on earth. I intentionally use the word* co-creation *because Source has sent many etheric light beings as ambassadors from the higher realms to carry out the Divine Plan of creation with you. In the swirling energy of seventh dimension, these sacred color-coded patterns burst into joyous song! It is the heavenly song that propels these wondrous patterns into sixth dimension. They become, in sixth dimension, the pure geometric forms for creation in your world.*

All that is manifested in your world must first be conceived in sacred geometry. The sacred geometric forms take on a substance closer to physicality in fifth dimension so that you are more easily able to co-create your world and its transformation at that etheric level. All of these higher dimensions, then, interact and flow toward propelling creation within the Divine Plan to its needed destination for the well being and evolving of your sacred Mother Earth and all her beings. That creation is yours to care for in love and light.

The etheric beings who co-create your world with you do so in pure compassion and great joy. It is your charge to learn from them as you take your creation forward into higher-dimensional consciousness from whence it came. It is your charge to move toward Ascension in that pure compassion and great joy! You are loved beyond measure by your brothers and sisters in the higher realms. We are with you each day in your great journey of love.

Dimensions ten, eleven, and twelve in our world move beyond the physical realm and connect us with the galactic level of consciousness. Even though we, as residents of the earth, do not live in these higher realms in our everyday lives, it is important for us to access the energy available to us from our galaxy for our continued evolution. That energy closely connects us to beings of light in other star systems in our galaxy. They are there to support us as we come together and heal with the earth.

We need the energy of all twelve dimensions, as does the earth, in our journey back to Divine Source. We can access that energy in many ways in our daily lives. Prayer and meditation can connect us to fourth, fifth, sixth, and even higher dimensions. Art, music, and just being in nature can also take us to these same dimensions. Giving and receiving Reiki connects us with all twelve dimensions by bringing Universal Life Force Energy through our galaxy and solar system for use in healing and evolution.

> *Our universe supports Mother Earth,*
> *as it supports all beings living on her,*
> *by continually sending multi-dimensional*
> *sacred life force energy into her*
> *etheric body or aura.*

Connecting with Mother Earth and all of the dimensions available to us through her is essential to our evolving in this lifetime with her. An important way of connecting with our earth and accessing the energy of the twelve dimensions is to visit the sacred sites of the earth. These special locations on the earth are places in which higher-dimensional energy can easily be accessed in third dimension. They are usually located at points where ley lines intersect in vortexes, especially where the telluric energy of water, mountains, or minerals provide a natural conduit for higher energy to flow.

Each sacred site on the earth has its own unique configuration of energy coming in from dimensions higher than the third dimension. For example, because of the flow of telluric energy on ley lines near flowing water and because of the location of vortexes, some areas in and around Sedona are filled with fourth, fifth, and sixth dimensional energy. Many people are drawn to this special location on Mother Earth to connect and interact with its unique sacred energy. Feeling this connection with sacred sites helps both humans and the earth evolve and move into the Age of Light through the love energy that is created by their interaction.

In the summer of 2000, I led a tour to the sacred sites of southern England to celebrate the Millennium. The trip was conceived when I was guided by my Higher Self to take people to the small town of Glastonbury where they could visit numerous sacred sites and connect with a major portal and chakra for our planet. As the plans became more concrete, I was also drawn to visit four other sacred sites. The trip came to include two ancient stone circles, Stonehenge and Avebury, as well as two churches, Wells Cathedral and Salisbury Cathedral. We would stay in a country cottage within reasonable driving distance from all sites. The goal for our trip was to feel our connection with the flowing spiritual energy of these sacred locations on Mother Earth and to thank her by allowing love energy to flow between us.

When we entered the town of Glastonbury, I felt a combination of deep joy, great warmth, and great sadness. These emotions came rushing in before we visited any of the major sacred sites of the area. I knew I was feeling the vortex energy and the energy coming in from the fourth, fifth, and sixth dimensions. I was moved to tears of joy even while the sadness remained with me. It came to me at that moment that I had lived at least one lifetime in that area. The combination of emotions seemed to be coming from that lifetime and from the great energy of the area in present time.

Higher-dimensional energy easily brings up emotions within human beings that need to surface for healing. Allowing ourselves to spend time with the energy of the sacred sites helps us evolve more quickly than most of us do in our everyday lives. This happens because of the feelings of connection. We receive from these holy sites the higher-frequency energy needed to open our hearts to spiritual experience, and we give back to these powerful sacred sites the love and presence we feel in that experience. We leave with them our energy combined with theirs, which will be used for the healing and evolving of the earth.

In Glastonbury we visited a number of sacred sites, including the powerful Tor, the Abbey, and the Chalice Well. These sacred sites, together with others in Glastonbury, form the heart chakra of Mother Earth. One of our purposes in visiting there was to feel the connection between our hearts and Mother Earth's heart chakra, in order to heal ourselves and her.

The Tor, an 800-foot tall hill towering over the town, has been a sacred site for at least 12,000 years. A vortex at the top of the Tor has been the location of a stone circle and a Christian church, both built over the powerful telluric energy of the area. I very much wanted to climb the Tor as the pilgrims of the past and present have done. I wanted to walk the labyrinthine path amidst the tremendously powerful ley lines winding up the slopes, but my fear of heights kept me from even attempting the climb.

Five years later, however, I returned to Glastonbury and finally climbed the Tor all the way to the top! As I climbed, I felt my Higher Self and the powerful telluric energy strengthening my body, my emotions, and my mind so that I could push through all the symptoms of my fear. I was able to do this in spite of a gusty wind that gave me an eerie sensation of being pushed off the narrow trails. I inched my way forward, somehow knowing that I would be held and protected all the way to the top.

The energy at the top was a reward I will always treasure. I felt at one with all those who made the Tor their place of connecting to Divine Source for millennia: Atlantean and Druid priests and priestesses, Pagans and Christians, pilgrims and visitors alike. Archangel Michael's presence was unmistakable, and I know that he joined that day with the powerful ley energy to carry me up that path! I was moved to tears of gratitude and joy to be in such a holy place on sacred Mother Earth. The experience was life changing for me. From that day onward I knew that I would always be lifted up.

*Connecting with Mother Earth
and all of the dimensions
available to us through her
is essential to our
evolving in this lifetime with her.*

In the summer of 2003, I led a tour to sacred sites in Scotland, including Loch Lomond, the Isle of Iona, Temple Wood Stone Circle, Kilmartin Standing Stones, and other standing stones in the district of Argyll. The goal for the trip was again to feel our connection with these holy beings on Mother Earth, to thank them for their light in our lives, and to leave our own light with them.

During that tour, Jann had an experience of feeling her connection with higher-dimensional energy that was life changing for her. When Jann entered the Temple Wood grounds, the first thing she noticed was a soft, exceptionally clear light shining on the stone circle. At first, she thought it was just the way the clouds were positioned at that time of day. Intuitively she walked counter-clockwise around both the outside and the inside perimeters of the stone circle. She then sat on a fallen stone where she could see, at the center of the circle, a cairn (burial site) created from a mound of stones. As she sat meditating, looking at that center monument, the light again was uniquely clear and soft. As she described it, it seemed like "light from another world or another time." She felt that time stood still in that circle.

It was in that moment that Jann realized that she had been there in a previous lifetime. She felt like crying, filled with emotions of sadness and overwhelming relief to know why she had come on this special journey. She was filled with the realization from her Higher Self that healing whatever painful experiences had happened in that lifetime would bring healing and growth to her present lifetime.

Later in the tour, Jann was able to see much more about the lifetime near Temple Wood. She was the daughter of the clan leader in that region of Argyll. When her father died, she was devastated and died soon afterwards in a state of mourning and fear. When her soul left her body, her father took her in his arms and carried her to a standing stone near Temple Wood. He showed her the writing etched in the stone and explained the true meaning of its symbolism. He told her that life does not end with the transition called death and that there was nothing to fear.

On hearing these words, Jann was able to completely release the fear she had felt at the time of death in that lifetime. This freed her to begin healing painful experiences she had in relationships in that lifetime. She realized that many of those same people were with her again in this lifetime. Since that trip she has been able to heal the relationships in present time by healing old pain from that distant past.

At Rancho La Puente, our healing center in New Mexico, there is a ley line running in front of our home along a path of underground water. The water and the ley line flow in a direct line from the barns of the back property, past our house, moving to the front land. The ley line is strengthened by our close proximity to Escudilla Bonita Volcano and large deposits of quartz, both clear and milky quartz, as well as amethyst. We are located close to Coyote Creek, with its generous underground water flow. People who come for retreats and Reiki healing circles remark about the peace and serenity they feel as soon as they drive onto the land.

All of our land also lies within a large vortex that is centered 20 miles to the northwest of Rancho La Puente. It is an electromagnetic vortex with great spinning action that brings in tremendous higher-dimensional energy for healing and releases toxins for the cleansing of Mother Earth and all beings living on her. We live in one of the arms of the vortex, and all of us at Rancho La Puente feel the intense higher-dimensional healing and cleansing energy. Within this large vortex is a smaller vortex on the land that we honor as a sacred site. We gather there during our retreats to connect with Mother Earth through meditation and rituals of healing.

Near Rancho La Puente is also a sacred site called The Petroglyphs. It is a natural formation of large rocks with a pool of spring water contained in their protective arms. On the rocks, beautiful petroglyphs (symbols) were carved by Native American shamans, depicting the people's relationship to the earth. The vortex energy creates the feeling of a protective womb there where fourth-, fifth-, and sixth-dimensional energies are easily accessed and utilized for meditation and healing.

Victor has led many spiritual ceremonies in this sacred environment using the higher-dimensional energy of Mother Earth for healing. Through allowing that energy to permeate his being, he has connected with a past life as a Native American on this land. He received a deep knowingness that he is back here again to complete the work he began at that time. That work is his life purpose in this lifetime.

Connecting with the higher-dimensional energy at sacred sites can bring us to a deeper understanding of our individual and collective life purpose on earth.

As we move into higher consciousness with the earth and all earth beings, we also open ourselves to Mother Earth's tremendous abundance. Her abundance comes from the pure crystalline white light of the ninth dimension. We access that abundance as we feel connected to and honor Mother Earth. We can do this by participating with sacred sites in any part of the world. We can either travel to those sites in person or feel our connection with them in meditation.

Another important way to feel connected to the crystalline energy of abundance is through sharing and service. It is the way of the higher dimensions brought to the earth during its creation and birth. Many civilizations have lived out of alignment with that Divine way over the millennia, but sharing and service have continued to exist in small pockets of Mother Earth's population. Today it is imperative that we all relearn this way of feeling our connection with the Divine Plan in order to survive, heal, and move into the abundance that is our birthright as earth beings.

*As we move into higher consciousness
with the earth and all earth beings,
we also open ourselves to Mother Earth's
tremendous abundance.*

Debbie had always dreamed of visiting the sacred sites in Europe and in the United States. In her mid-30s, she was able to travel to a number of sacred sites in the United States, including Sedona, Canyon de Chelly, and Mount Shasta. She was filled with awe and higher-dimensional energy at each site and decided to visit sacred sites in Europe during the next 10 years.

When she was 38 years old, she married Jim, a man who was 21 years older than she was. He was excited to share in her travels to European sacred sites. In their first year of marriage, they traveled to the Isle of Iona in Scotland, Glastonbury in England, and to several cathedrals in Italy. Their travels then came to an abrupt stop when both of their mothers became extremely ill. Debbie's mother, Elaine, was diagnosed with a debilitating disease, and Jim's mother, Janice, had complications from a stroke. Neither woman could live on her own at that time.

The couple decided to become the primary caregivers for both mothers. Both Elaine and Janice were very happy to live with Jim and Debbie. Jim's father had died when Jim was a child and Debbie's parents were divorced. The couple's siblings lived far from them and agreed to visit when they could but could not help on an ongoing basis. The couple agreed that this was the service and sharing they were supposed to do at this time in their lives. Both were self-employed and created ways to schedule their time so they could be at home part of each day with their mothers. They also found two outside caregivers to be there part of the time so they could have needed alone time and time with each other.

Jim and Debbie also agreed that since they could not travel to sacred sites at that time, they would connect with these sites through meditation and through sharing the energy of the sites with their mothers. Each morning before beginning their day, Jim and Debbie meditated together whenever possible. They felt connected in this way to sacred sites in the United States, Europe, and Latin America. They found themselves moving more quickly on their path to Ascension by feeling these connections as well as by the service and sharing they felt was their higher purpose.

Jim and Debbie received the abundance that comes from connection to the earth and to the higher dimensions. They felt the flowing of the fourth dimension and the creativity and expansion of the fifth dimension. Their businesses prospered and their relationships with their mothers grew closer than ever before. Their relationship with each other moved to a deeply spiritual place, and they easily shared their love with others in both personal and business relationships.

We can honor sacred Mother Earth wherever we are on her surface. We do not need to travel to sacred sites in order to give her the honor that is her due. Sacred sites are special places that make it easier for us to connect with her in her multidimensional glory. They maintain the ongoing flowing of energies coming in from dimensions 4 through 12 through the portals and vortexes of the earth. Every spot on the earth, however, is a sacred place. On sacred ground, we can participate in growing and conserving earth's beauty and bounty. We can grow our own food or participate in organic food exchanges. We can participate in clean water and clean air efforts.

We can honor the earth by creating rituals and ceremonies to thank her for the abundant gifts of water, air, soil, food, shelter, and beauty. Indigenous peoples have honored Mother Earth in this manner for eons. The earth receives our gratitude and sends even greater abundance. Rituals and ceremonies of connection and gratitude can be created alone or with others. It is wonderful to express them outdoors where all your senses can connect with Mother Earth and the sun that sustains her.

Rituals can include holding the sacred soil of Mother Earth in your hands, asking her to heal and cleanse you as you connect to her. It is very helpful to sit or lie on her ground as you thank her for each of the abundant gifts that she continues to give you each day. You can thank Mother Earth for the water, the air, the sun, and the food that give life to you and to all earth beings. You can thank the earth for helping you connect with your Higher Self in this lifetime.

Your ritual can include telling Mother Earth that you desire to move into higher consciousness with her during these sacred years before 2012. It is important in any ritual or ceremony to have some quiet time to just be with her, receiving her energy into your body, emotions, mind, and spirit. Then you can send your energy out to her in a circling flow of energy between you. You can tell her that you will continue to send and receive energy with her in your everyday life.

Mother Earth and all beings living on her are moving quickly now into the Age of Light. As multi-dimensional beings, we humans are learning to feel our connection to Mother Earth more profoundly than ever before. As we learn to honor our relationship with her through ritual, meditation, sharing, and service, we will live in the crystalline abundance that is our birthright as her children.

FOR REFLECTION

1. See Appendix B for a list of some sacred sites. Do you feel drawn to visit any of these or other sacred places on Mother Earth? If you are unable to visit them in person, you can use the meditation at the end of this chapter to connect with them wherever you are.

2. Set aside a special time to honor Mother Earth. Create your own ritual alone or with others. After this special time, write about your experience and share it if you wish.

MEDITATION
CONNECTING WITH A SACRED SITE

Find a comfortable place to sit or lie, either outdoors close to the earth or in a room where you feel peaceful. Plan a time when you can be alone there for at least 20 minutes.

1. Choose a sacred site that you feel drawn to for this meditation. If you do not have a particular location in mind, you can choose from Appendix B. Just scan the list with your inner vision and choose the one that holds the greatest light for you at this time.

2. Close your eyes and breathe deeply for a short while, allowing yourself to relax into the present moment... ask your Higher Self to be with you to connect with the sacred site you have chosen today...allow yourself to see or sense the sacred site, to feel the energy of the site... allow its energy to flow into your entire being.

3. Ask the sacred site what message it has for you today. The answer may come in words, a picture, colors, or a sensing. If the answer does not come during the meditation, trust that it will come at the exact right time for your life.

4. Thank the sacred site for being with you today, and send love energy from your heart to the consciousness of this wondrous place on Mother Earth...just be with those feelings of love for the next few moments...allow yourself to slowly come back to present time, taking the gifts you have received into your daily life.

CHAPTER NINE

MOVING TO ASCENSION

Long before we became incarnated on this earth, we lived in oneness with Divine Source. As human beings here on earth, we are still connected in that oneness. Feeling that oneness or connectedness again is the path back to Divine Source. That path takes us into higher and higher consciousness until our bodies become bodies of light. The moment we become a body of light is the moment of Ascension. Ascension is a great spiritual leap on the path of all beings as they move back to Divine Source. There are many spiritual leaps after that moment, but all of us who live in third dimension look toward Ascension as a decisive and glorious graduation from our earth school. From that moment on, we are free to live in higher-dimensional consciousness with or without physical bodies.

On the evolutionary path to Ascension, we take initiations or leaps of consciousness. For human beings, there are six major spiritual leaps or initiations on that path. In the past, it could take many, many lifetimes to take the first major leap, or First Initiation, but we were always moving in that direction. Today things are very different. An evolutionary leap that took many, many lifetimes in the relatively recent past can take just months now.

Ascension is a great spiritual leap
on the path of all beings as they move back
to Divine Source.

We and Mother Earth are going through a tremendous spiritual transition at this time. We are preparing for a huge leap in consciousness that has never happened before. Many planets in many solar systems have ascended to higher consciousness, and many individuals on those planets have ascended over the millennia. What is so different for us now is that the higher collective consciousness of all of Mother Earth's people has asked for the chance of ascending at the same time Mother Earth ascends. This higher collective consciousness is that part of all of us together that remains in higher consciousness while our soul extensions are having a third-dimensional experience here on earth.

In Amorah Quan Yin's landmark book, *The Pleiadian Workbook*, she presents information channeled to her by Ra, who is the spokesperson for the Pleiadian Emissaries of Light and the Archangelic Tribes. Ra helps us understand what is so different now in our world and in the universe.

Ra reminds us that we are coming to the end of three cycles in our universe, which simultaneously take place at the end of 2012. Our sun and entire solar system are coming to the end of a 26,000-year cycle of orbiting Alcyone, the central sun of the Pleiades (we are the eighth sun out in the Pleiades). At the same time, the entire Pleiadian system (including our solar system) is at the end of a 230,000,000-year cycle of orbiting the Galactic central sun, and our entire galaxy is completing a multi-billion-year cycle of orbiting the Great Central Sun of our universe.

The convergence of the end of these three major cycles means that all negative energy accumulated within ourselves, our civilization, and our planet must be cleansed as we move into the next major cycles. We must release all dark, destructive forces that still control so much that is happening on earth today. Once that cleansing has taken place, Mother Earth and all of the beings on her will move into fourth-and fifth-dimensional consciousness.

Ra presents four principles for human beings to embrace in order to live on the earth in higher consciousness:

> "By the year 2013, everyone who remains on Earth must understand the following four evolutionary principles: (1) The human purpose on Earth is to evolve physically, emotionally, mentally, and spiritually. (2) Every human being has a Divine Essence made of light and love whose nature is goodness. (3) Free will is an absolute universal right; impeccability calls on the self to surrender its free will to divine will in faith and trust. (4) All of natural existence is sacred beyond how it serves or meets the needs of the individual self."
> (*The Pleiadian Workbook*, p. 43)

Every human being on earth is now being presented with these principles through their Higher Selves. The principles are being presented in either subtle or direct ways. Some direct ways they are being presented are through spiritual classes, books, and messages from angels and Ascended Masters. Indirect but very intense ways in which to learn these principles include the experience of serious accidents, illnesses, or near-death experiences. More subtle ways these principles are revealed are through movies or day-to-day interaction with other people.

We have tremendous help right now. The Spiritual Hierarchy of this planet is assisting us. The Spiritual Hierarchy includes all those who have already ascended from the earth, the Ascended Masters. The head of the Spiritual Hierarchy is Lord Maitreya, who has many Ascended Masters under him who have specific important duties to perform at this time. A great number of those masters were in the spiritual realms until recently, but they have now taken on physical bodies and are present on the earth. They are not yet widely known, but they will make themselves known after Lord Maitreya announces himself to the entire population of the earth.

Lord Maitreya is living in London at the present time and is teaching in Hindu temples. However, he bilocates and appears to people in many countries who are ready to see him. When he makes himself widely known, he will present the evolutionary principles in person.

Those who choose not to embrace these evolutionary principles will need to move on to another third-dimensional planet in another area of the galaxy. Those who do choose to embrace the principles can move into fourth dimension with our planet. And those who ascend will move into fifth dimension. Those who ascend can either choose to stay on the earth in their Lightbodies to serve our planet or move on to other work in the higher dimensions.

Besides all the Ascended Masters who are helping us, our space brothers and sisters, especially from this galaxy, are here to help us as well, either in spirit or many times in earth bodies. The Pleiadians, especially, have a great interest in helping us because the earth and our solar system are part of the Pleiadian star system. All of the other solar systems in the Pleiadian star system have moved into higher consciousness. The Pleiadians are our very close relatives, and they want us to be with them in the light.

The Galactic Federation is made up of representatives from all the planets and solar systems in this galaxy that are living in higher consciousness. Some are here on earth helping us now. Others are helping us spiritually from their home planets and from their spaceships. They are waiting for Lord Maitreya to make himself known. Then they will physically come to help us.

The angels and the Archangels are also helping us, each in the special ways directed by Divine Source. Archangel Metatron, for example, is helping us build more light within our bodies. Archangel Michael provides us with help to speak our truth and release all that is not of the highest truth.

Angels surround all of our activities, urging us to connect with our Higher Selves in our daily lives. They light the way when we reach out to people, to animals, and to the earth. We feel their presence in our lives as soon as we open our hearts to them.

We and Mother Earth are going through a tremendous spiritual transition at this time.

In order to understand our part in the process of Ascension, it is important to look at the beginning of creation. At the beginning, Divine Source created an infinite number of individual sparks of Divine energy in a spiritual state. These individual Divine sparks are called monads. In order to experience a denser form of energy, each monad created 12 souls. Each soul, in order to experience an even denser form of the material universe, created 12 soul extensions, or personalities. These soul extensions could then incarnate on the earth and on other planets in third dimension. We each belong to a soul family of 12 and a monadic family of 144.

Each monad continually sends life force energy to its souls and its soul extensions. That spiritual energy gives us life and expresses the purpose of the Divine Plan within us. As we receive and respond to that energy in each lifetime, we are strengthened and guided on our journey back to Divine Source. Ascension is the greatest leap we can take on earth during that journey back to Divine Source.

Initiations are major steps we each take on our way to Ascension. As we prepare for these steps, we move from being immersed in material life to beginning to feel connected to spirit. That movement can take many lifetimes and include many negative and positive experiences. Today, however, human beings are taking these steps at lightening speed.

The big lesson for the First Initiation is the balance of the physical body. At this initiation, we understand that we are not our bodies. It is the beginning of Christ consciousness, which is the consciousness of responsibility, unconditional love, and service. All who take this initiation have a unique shift of consciousness, moving from being absorbed in physicality to feeling connected to their souls.

Roberta prided herself on her youthful, strong body. She worked out for long hours at the gym to maintain her appearance and thought of herself as the person she saw in the mirror. She never wanted to get pregnant because she knew she would lose her youthful body.

After some time had passed in her marriage, Roberta felt a growing desire to seek spiritual answers in her life. At the same time, she began to look at pregnancy as the potential of having a relationship with another small human being. She was still resistant to doing anything that would change her body, but gradually the desire to have a child became greater than the fear of losing her youthful body.

Roberta's First Initiation took place the moment she finally made the conscious decision that she would have a child. She released the extreme attachment to the looks of her physical body and finally felt connected to her soul. She expressed it as a surrender of her body. She knew that the baby came first and that her identity included far more than just her body.

The big lesson for the First Initiation is the balance of the physical body.

The big lesson for the Second Initiation is balance of the emotional body. At this stage, we learn that we are not our emotions. It used to take many, many lifetimes to move to this initiation because it is so difficult as human beings to release our emotional attachments. At this initiation, ego desires begin to be replaced by spiritual desires, and connection with the soul takes a big leap.

As we move toward taking the Second Initiation, we learn to fully feel our negative feelings, acknowledge them, let them move through us, and then release them. Most of us carry unresolved emotions for eons before resolving and releasing them at this initiation.

Many times the emotions that come up at this time are the ones we are most ashamed of or that we have kept secret. Anger, depression, and childhood pain often come up in the circumstances of our daily life to be released at this time. It usually takes some huge loss to finally let go and take the Second Initiation. It is most often a loss concerning people.

Anne was a woman in her late 40s who married as soon as she graduated from high school. The young man she married had been with her in several previous lifetimes, and the relationship they had in those lifetimes was a mixture of deep love and extreme hatred. They brought the karma between them into this lifetime to heal. Anne and her husband had two children and remained married in this lifetime for 15 years. During the last three years of their marriage, Anne's husband had affairs with three other women and finally left to marry one of them. Anne was devastated when he left and at first believed that he would come back. She struggled with all of the same emotions that she had experienced in one of their previous lifetimes together. Her anger, depression, and feelings of hopelessness were so strong that she could not emotionally release him.

When it was evident a few years later that her ex-husband was not going to return, Anne thought that at least they could be friends because of their children. She again struggled with all of the same emotions even though she had begun releasing parts of the old relationship. During that time, Anne went to therapy and began releasing many other old emotions connected to childhood and to other people. She was well on her way to her Second Initiation.

The crisis that brought her to her Second Initiation was the day she learned that her ex-husband and his new wife were going to have a child. Anne plunged more deeply into depression than she had when he first left the marriage. She realized that a friendship with him was unrealistic.

Her hopelessness seemed to envelop her completely. She came to me for Reiki healing at that time, and it was during one of the Reiki sessions that a huge shift came. Through visualization, Anne spoke to her ex-husband during the session and was able to release her old pain about their relationship from her physical body and her emotions. It was the moment of her Second Initiation.

At the Second Initiation, we balance our emotional body.

The Third Initiation has to do with balance of the mental body. At this initiation our personalities become merged with our souls; we purify our mental bodies and are responsive primarily to ideas and intuitions coming from the soul. We are no longer controlled by our lower minds, so we are free to release those ego-controlled thought patterns that we have carried for eons. We finally let go of our biggest illusions— illusions about how life and relationships should be. We release old negative beliefs about ourselves and others, about change, and about death.

William was a man in his 60s who was considered to be a very intelligent and intellectual person by his friends. He had been moving on the path of initiation for his entire adult life and was very conscious of the exact moments he had taken his first two initiations. The Third Initiation was more difficult for him than the others because he prided himself on his "thinking powers." While his logical thought patterns were very helpful in his work in the aerospace industry, many of his thought patterns were self-defeating in his personal life.

William went through his Second Initiation at the time of his divorce. He released the tremendous emotional pain of losing a relationship with the woman he still loved. He did not, however, release his long-held belief in the way marriage should be. He believed that marriage should be for life, no matter what the circumstances of individual couples may be.

William's wife told him that she never really loved him as a spouse and had only married him to be able to stay in the United States. She said that she loved him only as a friend and, after seven years of being together, wanted her freedom to find someone else. William believed that if all she felt was friendship, then friendship would have to be enough for both of them. He held to his belief that they were married for life.

As he moved closer to his Third Initiation, William struggled with releasing his long-held illusions. It was not until his sister, Maggie, left a marriage of 25 years that he was able to even look at the possibility that his belief about marriage was an illusion. After she left her husband, Maggie lived with William for six months. She talked and cried with him many evenings when he came home from work. Maggie became suicidal at one point, and William helped her get professional assistance and was very supportive through her crisis. Maggie's crisis provided the circumstances for William to come to his own crisis point in which he finally released his illusion about marriage. He took his Third Initiation at the point when he made that leap.

We let go of our biggest illusions at the time of our Third Initiation.

The Fourth Initiation is known as the Initiation of Renunciation. It has to do with freedom from self-interest and also with the releasing of attachments. Each of us has our own greatest challenges in releasing attachments, depending on what we are clinging to in third dimension. This may include attachments to people, to reputation, to money, and to things. But most of all it includes attachment to negative ego.

Our souls merge back into the monad at this initiation. We feel our spiritual oneness with our monad, and our guidance from this point forward comes directly from the monad. Until that time, our souls have guided us, so we experience a deep sense of loss when we no longer need the guidance from our souls. It takes time—sometimes several months—for most of us to become aware of our monads guiding us. When we do finally feel the energy of our monads, we also begin to experience the freedom that comes from no longer being controlled by our personalities. Our focus becomes one of service to the Divine Plan.

Danielle was a Reiki Master-Teacher in California who felt called to move her Reiki practice to another state. She had felt nudgings in that direction for several years but had been hesitant to move because she had lived in California her entire life and felt very comfortable there. She felt the calling in a very strong way when she visited a sacred site in the southern part of the United States and knew that she needed to take her healing practice to that area.

Danielle knew she was called to serve in this new part of the United States even though she did not know why. She had taken her Third Initiation earlier that year and had released the illusion that she could not make enough money living anywhere except California. Leaving the home she had always known, however, still felt like a tremendous loss to her. As she began to find out more about the new area where she had decided to live, she had a growing sense of insecurity and doubt about the step she was about to take.

Danielle moved ahead anyway, traveling a number of times to the new area. She found a home to buy that could serve very well as an office and a place to live. In order to make it happen, she would have to use most of her savings plus the proceeds from the sale of her home in California. Danielle began feeling a tremendous loss about the money she had taken many years to save as well as tremendous fear that she would not be able to get enough clients to support herself in her new home.

She came to me for Reiki sessions to work on those feelings of fear. During those sessions, she realized that she was moving closer to her Fourth Initiation because she had many periods of time when she was overwhelmingly sad. She was grieving losses not only of her home and money and security, but she also felt a crisis in her identity as a Reiki Master-Teacher. She knew that she was supposed to do healing work in the new location but she had no idea if she could find students for her Reiki classes there. She began to feel like she was losing everything. Everywhere she turned she saw more loss.

During the Reiki sessions, Danielle realized that she was resisting taking her Fourth Initiation. She was afraid that it would be a horrible experience with more loss and pain. As she was receiving Reiki one day, she finally said out loud that she was willing to take the step in spite of the fear. As soon as she said those words, she said, "I feel something like a vacuum over my mouth!" She took a small gasp and whispered, "My soul has returned to the Monad." She had stepped through the initiation. The loss and pain did not come with the moment of the initiation. It came in the life crisis she had been experiencing before that moment.

The Fourth Initiation frees us from self-interest to focus on the Divine Plan.

At the Fifth Initiation, we consciously merge with our monads. We are liberated to see a new vision. It is the vision of deeply understanding oneness. The person who has taken this initiation looks at the world and thinks, "I am the running river. I am the mountain peaks. I am the singing birds. I am the frightened deer." They also look at the world and think, "I am my sister. I am my father. I am the hungry people. I am the baby being born." This person knows from the depths of their being that as we join together once again we will all come to that understanding.

The light that comes from seeing this new vision allows us to open our hearts to receive the tremendous energy of our monads to use for world service. At this point, we must move to complete our higher purpose or mission on earth. With each initiation, the light in our bodies increases. At the Fifth Initiation, our bodies become filled with light.

Mary Ann had been following the path of Ascension for many years. She had studied virtually all that was published about Ascension before the year 2000. She used the best of those writings for her daily meditation and prayer. She moved on her own spiritual path, sometimes with help from third-dimensional human teachers and always with the help of spiritual beings from the higher dimensions.

Mary Ann came to me as a Reiki student just before her Fourth Initiation. She had studied with another Reiki Master-Teacher for several years in the past, completing her first three Reiki classes with the other teacher. Mary Ann loved and admired the other teacher very much, and when the teacher died a few years ago, it had been one of the greatest losses that propelled her toward her Fourth Initiation. She knew that

Reiki was paramount on her path of Ascension, so she began looking for a new teacher. When she came to one of my Reiki Healing Circles, she decided to study with me. She took her Fourth Initiation while receiving Reiki during her Reiki Master-Teacher class.

After her Fourth Initiation, Mary Ann began seeing me for spiritual guidance and Reiki sessions. She began her movement toward the Fifth Initiation. She continued to feel many losses in her life as she had before her Fourth Initiation. It seemed that whatever she still needed to release presented itself to her. She had released attachments to people and money and reputation in order to take her Fourth Initiation, and yet more issues about money and reputation came up to be released. She worked with each issue on the Reiki table as well as in prayer, meditation, and through daily actions.

Mary Ann's greatest challenge came when she lost her job. She had been employed for many years by a non-profit agency that assisted the homeless. She loved her work and had created a number of innovative programs that greatly increased the quality of assistance available to the homeless in her part of the country. When the agency's major funding source did not renew their contract, the agency closed its doors and its employees lost their jobs.

As she looked for a job, Mary Ann realized it would be very difficult to find a similar position. Her glowing reputation among non-profit agencies did not help her to find employment. Within a few weeks, she realized that she must release not only her recently lost job but even potential work in her chosen field. It was a big loss, but she saw on the Reiki table that it was small compared to all that she had to release before her Fourth Initiation. She also saw that it was time for her to do different work on the path of her higher purpose in this lifetime. She prayed, meditated, and sent Reiki for clarity about her new work.

One day as she was meditating, Mary Ann felt herself filling completely with light, and the following words came to her whole being: "All is one. My monad and I are one. I am the homeless man and woman I helped. They are my monad—my mother and father in spirit!" She knew that this was her Fifth Initiation because she understood oneness now, not only intellectually and spiritually but from the depths of her being. She also understood fully that her new work would not be new at all but would be a continuation of her higher purpose on a wider scale.

A few days later, Mary Ann received a call from a business acquaintance, telling her of the availability of new grant money for assisting disenfranchised groups in the United States and in third-world countries. The business acquaintance urged her to write her own grant and to lead a new organization herself. She prayed and sent Reiki to the new possibility, and within three days she knew that this was the continuation of her mission on earth in this lifetime. She called a colleague who agreed to help her write the grant, and people soon called her, asking to be part of her new organization.

Mary Ann is now happily leading an organization dedicated to assisting disenfranchised groups in third-world countries to create and sustain cooperative ventures that bring them both income and leadership roles in society. Mary Ann is completing her work in world service as she moves toward her Sixth Initiation.

Fifth Initiation allows us to deeply understand oneness.

The Sixth Initiation is Ascension. We have already consciously and spiritually merged with our monads at Fifth Initiation. At the Sixth Initiation, we physically merge with our monads. At the moment of Ascension, our entire beings are turned into light—we now fully inhabit our Lightbodies. Our Lightbodies have been slowly created from the light we have manifested throughout the time we have incarnated in third dimension. At the very moment we move into our Lightbodies, we also physically merge with the light of our monads. We are then fully united with our monads once again.

In order to ascend, we must have completed our mission or higher purpose on earth. Up until very recent times, human beings who ascended passed on to the spiritual world. Today many Ascended Masters are choosing to stay on earth to continue their service. Since little has been revealed about how we can stay on earth when we move fully into our Lightbodies, I asked Lord Maitreya to give us more information: *It is important that human beings who hope to ascend during this special and glorious time understand that a new dispensation has been given. Until recent years persons who ascended filled fully with heavenly light either left the earth with their physical bodies or left their physical bodies on the earth, moving only in their glorious Lightbodies.*

In the new dispensation, many are staying on the earth after Ascension. They do not physically die but live on in their physical bodies joined completely with their Lightbodies. All are given the choice to stay in order to serve the earth or to move on to the higher realms to serve in other ways. Ascension is a natural, a graceful, and a glorious experience! We, your family, are with you to guide you, to love you, and to receive you as you make this wonderful journey! Allow this message to move out to many human beings so that more humans will be open to moving more quickly on this great journey!

If we choose to stay on earth in physical bodies after Ascension, we will probably serve in very similar ways as we served before, but we will take on new aspects of that service as needed by the world. We will live in total joy and total unconditional love. We will have the feeling of oneness at all times with all beings.

If we choose to stay on earth, we will be able to materialize or dematerialize ourselves as needed for our work. We will create all that is needed instantly, and we will be able to bilocate as needed in order to serve the world. Service is our only focus as Ascended Masters, whether on earth or in the spiritual realms.

We physically merge with our monads at the Sixth Initiation.

Long before we came to this earth plane of existence we lived in oneness with Divine Source. We chose to come to earth as part of our experience as soul extensions. Most of us forgot that total connectedness over eons of time. We remembered during some of our incarnations. We lived in deep illusion during many of our lifetimes. It is time now to release all illusion and move more quickly back to oneness with each other and with Divine Source. Ascension is the greatest spiritual leap that we can take while still here on earth. May we move together quickly now toward that glorious experience!

FOR REFLECTION

1. The second spiritual principle states that "Every human being has a divine essence made of light and love whose nature is goodness." In what areas of your life are you living that principle? Is there any area of your life in which you have not fully embraced that principle?

2. The third spiritual principle states that "Free will is an absolute universal right; impeccability calls on the self to surrender its free will to divine will in faith and trust." Impeccability means choosing right action in daily life. Are there any ways in which you want to choose right action more fully in your life at this time? How can you practice more faith and trust in your daily life?

MEDITATION
CONNECTING WITH YOUR PATH OF ASCENSION

To prepare for this meditation, find a place to sit where you will not be disturbed for at least 15 minutes. Have some paper and a pen near you.

1. Sit quietly for a few minutes, breathing deeply. Then ask your Higher Self to become more present to you now.

2. When you feel connected to your Higher Self, ask, "Where am I on my path toward Ascension?" Then ask, "Which initiation am I working on now?"

3. Sit quietly and allow a message to come from your Higher Self. Write down whatever comes to you.

4. Thank your Higher Self for what you have received and ask for continued help in moving to your next initiation.

5. Take the information you have received and reread the section about the initiation you are working on to help you see your next steps.

AFTERWORD

In order to ascend with Mother Earth, we are each responsible for completing our life purpose in this lifetime. Our unique purpose is always about bringing more light into the world. We bring that light into the world through feeling our connectedness with all beings.

Each chapter of this book presented a roadway to feeling connection within ourselves and with other beings. Healing our Inner Child allows us to know and love ourselves as we really are. Creating close relationships with our Higher Self and with spiritual light beings opens the way to feeling connected in the light at a higher dimensional level. Healing through human relationships helps us to feel connected at the third-dimensional level.

Healing our past lives helps us to release old patterns of relating that keep us from feeling united with our true selves and others. Animals teach us how to give and receive unconditional love in relationship. Feeling sacred earth energy brings us into direct contact with Divine Source in nature, and allows us to feel connected to Mother Earth's higher dimensional energy through which she will ascend. Reiki brings Spiritually Guided Universal Life Force Energy into every cell of our bodies and every part of our present and past lives to free us from all feelings of separateness.

It is our responsibility and our privilege as spiritual

human beings to share our radiant light with all other spiritual beings who join us on our third-dimensional journey. As we share our light with other humans, with animals, with all earth beings, and with Mother Earth herself, we move as one on the glorious path of Ascension that is our birthright and our deepest joy!

Marie Neumeier Rientord offers ongoing workshops, retreats, and classes at Rancho La Puente Healing Center in New Mexico and at other locations. For information about any of these events or about individual spiritual guidance and Reiki sessions, you can contact Marie at:

www.rancholapuente.com

Appendix A
Animal Gifts to Humans

Ants – connectiveness

Bats – adaptability

Bears – soul power, mother energy

Beavers – creativity, love of family

Bees – service

Birds

        cranes – solitude, independence

        crows – awareness, connectiveness

        doves – peace, harmony

        eagles – soul power, father energy

        hawks – passion for life

        hummingbirds – beauty, wonder, uniqueness

        jays – presence, confidence

        owls – wisdom, calirvoyance, patience

        pigeons – inner guidance

        ravens – clairvoyance

        swans – grace, balance

Buffalo – abundance, courage, healing

Butterflies – transformation

Cats – independence, intuition, play

Chickens – resourcefulness

Cows – love of family

Coyotes – balance, humor

Deer – love, gentleness, kindness

Dogs – love, loyalty, service

Dolphins – love, trust, supportiveness, play

Elephants – guardianship, connectiveness

Elk – strength, flexibility, freedom

Foxes – protection, passion

Frogs – abundance

Goats – resourcefulness, perseverance

Horses – enlightenment, freedom, strength

Mountain lions – leadership, courage

Mice – discernment

Rabbits – serenity, gentleness

Raccoons – curiosity, ingenuity

Rats – adaptability